The Politics
of Underdevelopment

GERALD A. HEEGER
UNIVERSITY OF VIRGINIA

The Politics
of Underdevelopment

St. Martin's Press • New York

In memory of Ralph Eisenberg

Preface

The study of underdeveloped political systems has undergone considerable change over the past several decades. The 1950's and early 1960's saw much theorizing—about the causes of underdevelopment, about the possibilities for development, about alternative strategies of development. Yet, while the various theories—structural-functional analysis, in particular—and the concepts they employed provided some initial direction for research, it was not long before scholars perceived that both the theories and the concepts were inadequate to explain political behavior in the underdeveloped state. Grounded in the Western political tradition, the various theories often distorted more than they explained.

Perhaps sensing the futility of attempts to develop comprehensive theory, many scholars turned their attention to the study of particular cases. In recent years there has been a virtual explosion of idiographic research on highly specific topics concerning the political systems of the underdeveloped states. Such things as local political systems, specific instances of public policy formation, and particular social and political changes within small groups have become the stuff of recent comparative political research. Such research has gone far in introducing us to the political systems of Africa and Asia.

This research alone, however, does not suffice for a general discussion of underdeveloped political systems. And because of the reluctance of scholars to attempt new general theories, outmoded ones continue to exert influence on research and to distort conclusions. The study of underdeveloped political systems has, so to speak, developed two languages. On specific problems, it uses sophisticated research techniques and astute descriptive analysis. For more general characterizations of political systems, the earlier theories and concepts, with which few were ever satisfied, persist. The enormous amount of data that has been collected in recent years seems to have had little impact on general theory.

This study is an effort to sketch some of the relationships which, in the light of available data, seem characteristic of underdeveloped political systems. It seeks, in other words, to frame theory in terms of data. But no all-encompassing "grand theory" is attempted: I have deliberately confined myself to seeking explanations for the continued incapacity of underdeveloped states to deal not only with the demands of modernization but also with the more limited problem of establishing some sort of political order in their societies. I have sought to challenge and reformulate some past and current theoretical conceptions.

Quite obviously, a little book which proposes to discuss a multitude of different political systems is an audacious undertaking. The list of individuals who have assisted me by their discussions and their own research—both published and unpublished—is too long to set down here. The footnotes in this book chronicle my intellectual debt to them.

I am deeply grateful to my colleagues in the Woodrow Wilson Department of Government and Foreign Affairs at the University of Virginia, especially to Alfred Fernbach, R. K. Ramazani, and Robert Wood, from all of whom I have learned a great deal. I would also like to express my appreciation to the University of Virginia for a grant which, in part, supported the research and writing of this study.

Finally, to my wife, Geraldine, who with encouragement and good humor has weathered my all too frequent moodiness during the work on this book, I can only express my gratitude.

G. A. H.

Contents

1

Political Underdevelopment
and the Search for Political Order

Politics in underdeveloped societies has become preeminently a politics in search of order. Development,
often an intangible concept at best, has proved to
be an elusive goal. Order, in contrast, is both more tangible
and, so it seems, more necessary. The growing number of military regimes with their anachronistic, colonial-era-like preoccu-
pation with order is only one indication of this shift from the
politics of development to the politics of order. This concern
for order is a consequence of the failure of most underdeveloped
states to make more than merely incremental changes in their
societies. Underdevelopment threatens to become a permanent
condition rather than a transitory stage.

The Theory of Political Development

The shift from the politics of development to the politics
of order has been only tangentially recognized by most political
scientists. The focus of their attention continues to be the process of developmental change, the means by which political
development is achieved. They discuss development either as
a syndrome derivative from the Western experience—charac-

terized by a growing secularization, the differentiation of political roles and structures, the emergence of equality as an operative ideal of society, and the increased capacity of men to deal with their environment[1]—or as a process of institutionalizing organizations and procedures in order to enable them to become viable and persistent in a rapidly changing environment.[2] In either case, the contemporary situation in underdeveloped states is noted only in passing, and its events are explained simply in terms of the lack of those attributes that particular scholars assign to their concept of development.

The study of politics in the new nations has changed only slightly over the past decade and a half. Earlier studies attributed a particular political, institutional, and behavioral "pathology" to developed states and analyzed underdeveloped states in terms of "gaps" between their pathology and that of developed states.[3] Recent discussions, while more complex, continue to focus on a transition from underdevelopment to development and continue to explain politics in underdeveloped nations in terms of their lacking what is arbitrarily defined as modern. Underdeveloped states are instable and weak, so it is argued, because their political structures are neither institutionalized nor differentiated, because their political cultures are neither egalitarian nor secular, and because their capacity to influence their social environment is either limited or nonexistent. Underdeveloped states, to restate this argument, are underdeveloped.

Such explanations beg a considerable number of questions about underdeveloped states. Even if one accepts the proposition that the "pathology" of the developed state is an essentially correct description of Western nation-states (which is very much debatable), the description of the new states in terms of their "gaps" tells us only that these underdeveloped states *are different*. Defining underdeveloped states in terms of what they are not reveals very little about politics as it actually occurs in such states.

In part, this lack of theoretical focus on the politics of underdeveloped states is a remnant of an earlier optimism about

POLITICAL UNDERDEVELOPMENT

the ultimate destination of human history, an optimism that saw both modernization and democracy as almost inevitable. Both the optimism and the lack of focus on the politics of underdeveloped states have their origins in something more basic, however: the way in which modernization and social change have come to be understood.

To most modern scholars of the subject, social change is both inevitable and inevitably modernizing.[4] Although modernization is often defined as only one type of social change, for example, "the transformation of all systems by which man organizes his society—the political, social, economic, intellectual, religious, and psychological systems,"[5] the terms "modernization" and "social change" as they are used in analysis tend to blur together. Because traditional societies, by definition viewed as lacking adaptability, are perceived as societies that must inevitably crumble in the face of social change,[6] social change assumes an almost inevitable modernizing character. Even where this line of reasoning is criticized as depicting tradition and modernity too rigidly, those critics do not really challenge the inevitability of social change and of modernization.[7] While tradition is argued to be more adaptive than originally theorized, that adaptability has perceptible limits, and even the most adaptive tradition is almost inevitably undermined by social change.

These points are not made to attach an apparent unidirectionality to the modern understanding of social change.[8] In some ways, the argument is unchallengeable. Just as some day we shall all be dead, so some day most things will be different. There are problems, however, in viewing social change and, indirectly, modernization as being almost inevitable, for such inevitability causes the concept of political development to become defined very specifically. That is, political development is seen to be concerned not so much with *initiating change* (which is inevitable) as with *managing change*, with channeling change and its consequences.[9] In this view, the disorder that has become characteristic of the new states results from change that has gotten out of hand, from mismanagement, or, to utilize

3

a current expression, from breakdowns in modernization.[10] As we shall argue momentarily, such a perception of political development considerably understates the task that confronts the new states and is too limited in its explanation of the sources of disorder.

The conceptualization of political development as the management of change is reflected in the current emphasis on political institutionalization as the key index of development.[11] Political institutions are seen as lying at the core of the community—whether that community already exists or is only in process—providing integrating symbols, making goal choices for the community, and extracting the social compliance necessary to achieve the chosen goals. Political institutions are patterns of social interaction that have become stabilized; and, by providing rules of the game for group interaction and conflict, they foster the emergence of a civic society and a public interest. Institutions, in other words, manage group interaction. Accordingly, their absence means group interaction with no rules except those of self-interest.

The perception of social change and of modernization as being inevitable not only yields a somewhat restricted definition of political development, it also arbitrarily places limits on the time span of underdevelopment. If change is inevitably modernizing, then underdeveloped states must be transitory phenomena. Such states are, as a result, understood as "delayed" or "arrested" states that are to be characterized in terms of the "gaps" between their features and those of a modern state. The focus remains on defining modernization and development, and politics in the underdeveloped states continues to be discussed in terms of its deviance from those definitions.

The Political Process in Underdeveloped States

Despite theory or the lack of it, political modernization and development have proved elusive. The "gaps" between

POLITICAL UNDERDEVELOPMENT

developed and underdeveloped states seem to be widening—not simply because the former are developing at an ever increasing rate (which they are), but also because, as Samuel Huntington has pointed out, the latter are stagnating or "de-developing." Social change has been fitful. The result has been a transformation in the very goals pursued by underdeveloped societies. Survival itself has come into question. The larger goals of modernization and democracy have given way to a more fundamental search for political order.

Social change, far from being inevitable and ultimately modernizing, is sporadic, erratic, and unpredictable in its consequences. Fixity and a resistance to change seem to be as ubiquitous as change itself. Moreover, where social change has occurred, it not only has created the managerial problem of controlling it and its consequences but also has often limited the possibility initiating further change.

There is a tendency to discuss social change, at least in theory, in very holistic terms. That is, social change is depicted as the replacement of a whole social structure, which guides all spheres of activity in a particular society, by a new whole social structure. The critical development problem in this view is the construction of and inculcation into new, modern social and political institutions.[12]

Such an argument often tends to gloss over what one scholar has called the "dysrhythmic" nature of change.[13] Traditional societies are highly localized and are often affected by change at different rates. New nation-states are "constellations" of traditional societies, and the fact that some traditional societies in a particular area are affected by social change does not mean that all such societies are. Some are virtually unaffected; some, marginally affected; some, massively. Moreover, few social structures are wholly transformed. Social change can affect parts of a society (as well as different societies) at a differential rate.[14] Old and new can persist side by side. For example, a chief may lose much of his political authority but retain his position in the ritual and social hierarchies.

The erratic character of social change is perceptible in

other ways as well. For example, while the transition from traditional social patterns to modern social patterns is often depicted in terms of the emergence of social structures and institutions coterminous with the nation-state itself, social change often produces modern groups that may be as localized as their traditional counterparts. The emergence of small, urbanized middle-class groups, which will be noted in our later discussion on nationalism, is an example of this. Such groups may be very limited in membership and interests and only intermittently linked to other groups elsewhere in the territory. Social change, in other words, may not only not cause the demise of traditional forms of particularism, it may also create new particularisms.[15] Social change can function to strengthen particular traditional groups or to transform them into new kinds of social organization. In India, local subcastes are linked into broader caste identities and caste associations; in Africa, clans manifest themselves in tribal groups; in Southeast Asia, the patron-client bonds so characteristic of traditional society have restructured themselves and have assumed an increasingly important role in the new political system.

The persistence of particularism and localism being suggested here is not a new idea. As Edward Shils has stated:

> The constituent societies on which the new states rest are, taken separately, not civil societies and, taken together, they certainly do not form a single civil society . . . they lack the affirmative attitude toward rules, persons, and actions that is necessary for consensus. They are constellations of kinship groups, castes, tribes, feudalities—even small territorial societies—but they are not civil societies. The sense of identity is rudimentary, even where it exists. . . .[16]

What I want to emphasize, however, is that social change does not necessarily erode traditional institutions, and can, in fact, create a variety of new particularisms. Social change, in other words, may only further fragment the already fragmented new nation-state.

There is another point that must be emphasized here as

well. Students of the underdeveloped states tend to view particularism as simply traditional and, hence, as more or less given. That is, the form in which particularism manifests itself is decreed by tradition, and it is in terms of such givens that the problem of nation-building for any particular state must be assessed. For this reason, many scholars discussing such problems formulate what in effect are "check lists" of particularisms existing in a society.[17] The more persistent and severe the particularisms, it is argued, the less chance of success in nation-building.

Our brief discussion on social change, however, suggests that particularism is a far more complex phenomenon. Change can transform particularism, but it is likely to be particularism nonetheless. Modernization can, in fact, accentuate particularism by stimulating the emergence of groups that have sufficient numbers to threaten the viability of the state in which the groups exist. Moreover, though social groups and a person's position relative to them are basic to his understanding of his world and of his place in it, the various groups—whether traditional, neotraditional, or modern—do not have obvious and inevitable political interests and strategies. A group's definition of its own interests and, in fact, of its own identity can alter radically in changing political conditions. Group consciousness tends to be the product of political mobilization, and the definition of the group and of its interests after such mobilization may vary considerably from what might have been predicted simply on the basis of a survey of the social characteristics of its members.

The malleability of social and political particularism is being emphasized here because it points to another focus in underdeveloped societies—the modernizing elites. The term "modernizing elite" is a catchall term generally used to describe those who have come to view themselves as the heirs of the colonial government. The modernizing elites are not a distinct, cohesive social class; they are crisscrossed by ethnic and regional affiliations, kinship, age groups, and patron-client relationships. Yet, in a sense, these elites do comprise a ruling

7

class. Rather than being simply the recipients of demands from particular groups or spokesmen for highly articulated social interests, they tend to be initiators in the political process. The modernizing elites have considerable latitude in their efforts to build political institutions and organizations, and political institutions such as political parties are reflective of elite attitudes and aspirations. The social groups often discussed in terms of the persistence of primordial ties or in terms of other economic and social cleavages are often mobilized in response to actions taken by the elites. Politics in the underdeveloped states is focused around the political functioning of the elites, elite interactions with one another, and the effect of such interactions on nonelites.

The persistent social fragmentation in the new states, the elitist character of their politics, and the tendency for fragmentation to have political salience in response to elite actions and interactions all work to create a political process that cannot be defined simply as an uninstitutionalized one where group confronts group. The issue is not so much whether or not political organizations or procedures are institutionalized but rather their particular character, institutionalized or uninstitutionalized. Political institutions in the underdeveloped states—especially "national" institutions—tend to be highly segmentary.[18] Power and support tend to be localized, and political institutions and organizations are characterized by coalitions of semi-autonomous elites and groups at the local, regional, and national levels. The political process, as a result, is defined by the efforts of the elites to coalesce with one another in order to establish national institutions in the center of the new society, by attempts to enlist societal support and elites outside that center, by group and elite responses to policies and politics in the center, and by efforts of center elites to accommodate such responses when they are dissident.[19]

The development of national political institutions and political movements is, then, dependent upon the willingness and the capability of modernizing elites to coalesce with one another and interlink the various social fragments of the society. Their ability to do so is limited, for elites have a low level of political capacity at the center. Their resources are few. The economic pie is small and limits patronage; coercive means are costly and scarce. The result is chronically weak institutions which hinge on fragile bargaining relationships between elites in the center and the periphery. Modernizing elites seek to gain support for their programs (or for their opposition to government programs) and for themselves by seeking alliances with other elites and social groups. In underdeveloped states:

> Structures of power relationships are fragmented and compartmentalized. Primary groups, and ethnic groups or demographical classes are the dominant reference groups. . . . each leader is a bargainer with every other one, both for himself and his followers. . . .[20]

Immobilism is almost inherent in this process. Where coalitions have not been or cannot be organized, intra-elite conflict prevents any one elite from attacking the problems of social change. Where coalitions are organized, the elites involved are, by the nature of their alliances, inhibited from implementing policies that might challenge the position of their particular followers or coalitional partners. Weak institutions and coalitional politics, more often than not, perpetuate the status quo. Governments do not so much work as muddle through.

One additional point needs to be made here. Our discussion of modernizing elites has remained purposely general. No one set of elites—political, bureaucratic, military, or the like—has been emphasized. There is a tendency in American scholarship to view the various "actors" in a political system—political parties, bureaucracies, interest groups, the military—as discrete organizational entities. That is, they are seen as involving different sets of elites seeking to institutionalize different sets of procedures, rules, and goals. As a result, political events are often explained by reference to the various institutions and their relative organizational strength. For example, the bureaucracy becomes a dominant element in the system because it is well organized; the military intervenes because all civilian political institutions have either collapsed or become wholly disorganized. Such an assumption considerably overstates the distinctions between elites in new societies. The elites who assume the key positions in the political center are relatively few in number, and the institutions of the system tend to evolve in response to their decisions. National politics in the new states is principally focused around the effort of extending authority downward and outward from those elites who claim power. The central elites seek to penetrate their authority into society and to generate widespread acceptance of that authority. The elites can, if they so choose, build a variety of different institutions to facilitate this process.

The focus of such institution-building is governmental authority. Elites who occupy governmental offices possess at least some capability to dispense goods and services in the society. The availability of such power, in effect, structures the loose system of elites and groups, forcing them into various coalitional structures in an effort to gain access to and control of the government. The control of key governmental offices allows the ruling elites, if they desire, to build a political party in much the same way that political machines were built in American cities in the early part of this century. Elites can also frustrate the construction of such party institutions in favor of military or bureaucratic institutions. In part, such decisions reflect the background and socialization of the particular elites. In part, such decisions also reflect differing elite perspectives on politics in the new states.

In summary, politics in the underdeveloped states is not a matter of organized groups and institutions vis-à-vis one another. Rather, it is the politics of faction, coalition, maneuver, and personalism.

The Decline of Optimism: From the Politics of Development to the Politics of Order

While most of the theoretical material about political development continues to argue at least implicitly the inevitability of development and modernization, specific studies of the countries of Africa and Asia have shown a discernible shift in mood. Recurrent patterns of civil strife, apparently insoluble economic problems, and institutional instability have all taken their toll on the optimism that political scientists had been prone to express in the 1950's and early 1960's. Yet, the theories still color the way in which specific events are discussed, and they have often served to obscure the sources of instability. Despite the growing pessimism among political scientists, their conceptualizations about social change and about institutions make politics in the new states difficult to comprehend. Addressing this same point, one scholar has written:

> Too often the politics of new states have been described as if intentions were facts, as if the word had become flesh; the characterizations of political systems in Africa are based on images conveyed to the world by party leaders.[21]

The result has been conceptualizations of party organizations as highly sophisticated organizational weapons, of bureaucracies as "iron skeletons," and so on. Such conceptualizations defy comprehension in the face of the instability of the underdeveloped states.

However difficult it may be for political scientists to visualize the politics of order, the modernizing elites in the new states are quite aware of the shift. Whatever images they may try to convey to the outside world, the ruling elites have long since become aware that their limited resources and their fragmented institutions are making underdevelopment a chronic rather than a transitory ailment. In such a situation, remaining in power has become a precarious endeavor, and the attention of the elites has shifted from development and modernization to survival itself. The institutions in the new states do what they can do, and the best they can do is to survive. Development remains an enigmatic, elusive luxury. In a political system of weak institutions, shifting alliances, and unpredictability, order—even momentary order—has come to mean survival itself. It is accomplishment enough simply to muddle through.

NOTES

1. This is, perhaps, the most commonly expressed definition of political development (those who utilize this definition usually use "political development" and "political modernization" interchangeably). See, for example, James S. Coleman, "Introduction," in James S. Coleman, ed., *Education and Political Development* (Princeton: Princeton University Press, 1965), p. 15; Lucian Pye, *Aspects of Political Development* (Boston: Little, Brown and Company, 1966), pp. 45-48; Gabriel Almond and G. B. Powell, *Comparative Politics: A Developmental Approach* (Boston: Little, Brown and Company, 1966), pp. 299-332; and Claude E. Welch, Jr., "The Comparative Study of Political Modernization," in Claude E. Welch, Jr., ed., *Political Modernization* (Belmont, Cal.: Wadsworth Publishing Company, Inc., 1967), pp. 1-16.

2. See, for example, Samuel Huntington, *Political Order in Changing Societies* (New Haven: Yale University Press, 1968); S. N. Eisenstadt, "Institutionalization and Change," *American Sociological Review*, XXIV (April 1964), 235-247; and S. N. Eisenstadt, "Social Change, Differentiation, and Evolution," *American Sociological Review*, XXIV (June 1964), 375-387.

3. See, in particular, Lucian W. Pye, "The Non-Western Political Process," *The Journal of Politics*, XX, 3 (August 1958), 468-486. Another important typological study is Fred W. Riggs, "Agraria and Industria," in William J. Siffen, ed., *Toward the Comparative Study of Administration* (Bloomington: Indiana University Press, 1959).

4. For an excellent study of the Western understanding of social change, see Robert Nisbet, *Social Change and History* (London: Oxford University Press, 1969).

5. Manfred Halpern, "Toward Further Modernization of the Study of New Nations," *World Politics*, XVII, 1 (October 1964), 173.

6. See, for example, David E. Apter, *Ghana in Transition* (New York: Atheneum, 1963).

7. See Lloyd I. Rudolph and Susanne Hoeber Rudolph, *The Modernity of Tradition* (Chicago: University of Chicago Press, 1967), especially Part I; and Joseph R. Gusfield, "Tradition and Modernity: Misplaced Polarities in the Study of Social Change," *American Journal of Sociology*, LXXII, 4 (1966), 351-362.

8. Such a critique can be found in Nisbet, especially pp. 284-287.

9. This is most visible in the writings of Huntington, Eisenstadt, and Almond and Powell.

10. S. N. Eisenstadt, *Modernization: Protest and Change* (Englewood Cliffs, N.J.: Prentice-Hall, 1966).

11. Huntington makes an important contribution in his separation of political development from modernization. Modern and modernizing states, Huntington asserts, can change by losing capabilities (decay) as well as by gaining them (development). Development, in other words, is not irreversible. Modernization, however, appears to be very much irreversible in Huntington's analysis; and the conditions that lead to

decay are a result of the modernization process itself. "Social and economic change . . . extend political consciousness, multiply political demands, broaden political participation. These changes undermine traditional political institutions; they enormously complicate the problems of creating new bases of political association and new political institutions combining legitimacy and effectiveness" (p. 5).

12. For example, see Huntington.

13. C. S. Whitaker, Jr., "A Dysrhythmic Process of Political Change," *World Politics*, XIV, 2 (1967), 190-217.

14. For one of the best studies of "substructural" change and of the apparent contradictions that often result, see F. G. Bailey, *Caste, Tribe, and Nation* (Manchester, Eng.: Manchester University Press, 1960).

15. "Particularism" is best defined as the tendency on the part of a group to define its identity and interests in highly localized, exclusivistic terms. The word is frequently used as a euphemism for tradition. But as the text points out, so-called modern groups are often no less particularistic than traditional ones.

16. Edward Shils, "On the Comparative Study of the New States," in Clifford Geertz, ed., *Old Societies and New States* (New York: Free Press, 1963), p. 22.

17. For an elaboration on this argument, see Gerald A. Heeger, "Politics of Integration: Community, Party, and Integration in Punjab" (Ph.D. dissertation, University of Chicago, 1971), introduction.

18. On the concept of segmentation, see M. G. Smith, "On Segmentary Lineage Systems," *Journal of the Royal Anthropological Institute* 86 (1956), 39-80; Meyer Fortes and E. E. Evans-Pritchard, eds., *African Political Systems* (London: Oxford University Press, 1940); and A. W. Southal, *Alur Society* (Cambridge, Eng.: W. Heffer and Sons, Ltd., 1953).

19. The concepts of center and periphery are explored in Edward Shils, "Centre and Periphery," *The Logic of Personal Knowledge: Essays Presented to Michael Polanyi* (London: Routledge and Kegan Paul, 1961), pp. 117-130.

20. Leonard Binder, *Iran: Political Development in a Changing Society* (Berkeley and Los Angeles: University of California Press, 1964), p. 36.

21. Henry Bienan, *Tanzania: Party Transformation and Economic Development* (Princeton: Princeton University Press, 1970), p. 5.

2

Nationalism and Its Legacies

Until the 1950's, the study of nationalism was large-ly the province of historians. Nationalism was, so it seemed, a phenomenon of a particular historical epoch, one that was drawing to a close. Particular nationalisms were seen as unique responses to the intellectual milieu of that epoch and, for that reason alone, of interest only to the historian. In the past two decades, however, the study of nationalism has come to be seen as far more than a mere exercise of historical inquiry; the emergence of stridently nationalist states in Africa and Asia has given nationalism a relevance it has not had since the French Revolution.

Despite the numerous studies devoted to the subject, nationalism and its related concept of nationality remain elusive. From the often bewildering welter of ideas and definitions, however, it is possible to make two general statements about the modern understanding of nationalism. First, nationalism has come to be understood in terms of modernization and its con-sequences. Whether ascribed to the spread of ideas that have marked the growth of the modern world or linked to the spread of those conditions identified with modernity—i.e., the expansion of literacy, a money economy, widening communications, and urbanization—nationalism is seen as being a break with the old order. Second, linked as it is to the shattering of the old order, nationalism has come to be viewed more as an emotional response to the death of that order than as the spread of any particular set of ideas.

Both of these statements will be examined in considerable detail in this chapter. They are basic not only to the modern understanding of nationalism, especially its non-Western forms, but also to the current understanding of nationalist movements and of the political systems that evolved from those movements.

The Western View of Nationalism

Nationalism in the West has been traditionally understood as a set of ideas focused around the notion of the nation-state. As such, the study of nationalism has been principally the study of the transmission of that set of ideas from one individual or set of individuals to another.[1] As a set of ideas, nationalism was comprehensible in terms of an intellectual history of those ideas. More important, as a set of ideas, nationalism was more than a simple sentiment of belonging to a particular community.[2] Nationalism was concerned with the nature of the state itself and was linked to alternative conceptions of sovereignty, authority, and individual rights. Nationalism was viewed as being related to the larger question of the nature of the just political order, and individuals were linked to nations in terms of a shared understanding of what that just political order was to be.

In recent years this traditional approach to nationalism has been sharply criticized as yielding a far too abstract understanding of nationalism. Such a perception of nationalism, it has been argued, gives it few if any tangible roots in a society.[3] Concerned as it seemed to be with philosophies of state, the traditional approach was seen as providing little explanation of the relationship between the appearance of nationalism and the rapid social change that seemed always to accompany its appearance.

The reaction to the traditional approach to nationalism has

16

been an effort to understand, with empirical evidence, the conditions under which groups of people formed nation-states.[4] Karl Deutsch, emphasizing modernization and its concomitant widening patterns of communication, has argued that nationality is best understood in terms of "the ability to communicate more effectively, and over a wider range of subjects, with members of one large social group than with outsiders."[5] Deutsch charted the evolution of a "people" in terms of a growing complementarity of social roles, habits, and communication facilities and defined a "nation" in terms of the sovereignty of a people over their own land.[6] Nationalism is, then, the "will" toward sovereignty on the part of a people.[7] Nationalism and nationality are the outcome of a changing social environment.

The recognition of the role of social change in nationalism was not wholly new with Deutsch and those who have followed him. Most of the intellectual historians of nationalism have acknowledged the role of the "rising masses" in the nationalist era.[8] What is new, however, is that social change has become the very definition of nationalism. Social change, modernization in particular, and nationalism are seen as inseparable. While traditional scholars saw philosophers and politicians arguing over the nature of the correct political order and man's place in it, modern students see nationalism less as a set of ideas than as a sentiment engendered by the process of change. Nationalism is, in essence, a reflection of the process of change. If nationalism defines membership in a particular community—the "we" in the question "Who are we?"—that definition is made not in terms of a common perception of politics and the political order but in terms of a common heritage of social change. As such, nationalism is not to be understood in terms of its content. The important question is not *what* people believe but *who* believes it. The ideas espoused by any particular nationalism are only programmatic additives to a sentiment that emerges from an altered social and, hence, psychological environment. In the modern view, nationalism is, more than anything else, an emotional response to modernization itself.

17

The West and the Understanding
of Non-Western Nationalism

The linkage between modernization and nationalism has been even more prevalent in the study of nationalism in non-Western areas. Earlier studies of nationalism tended to view non-Western nationalism as distinctly different from its Western European counterpart, stressing the so-called "artificiality" of the new nations in Asia and Africa. More recent studies have tended to minimize such distinctions. While non-Western nationalism is generally differentiated in terms of the areas and cultures of its origins and in terms of its contemporary nature, it is viewed as being essentially the same phenomenon as Western nationalism. As Rupert Emerson has written:

> Nationalism wherever it manifests itself is in essence a response to the forces which in recent centuries have revolutionized the West and have penetrated in successive waves to the farthest corners of the world.[9]

The revolutionary force to which Emerson refers is modernization itself. Modernization is a process whereby "major clusters of old social, economic, and psychological commitments are eroded and broken" and new ones created in their place.[10] The development of any particular nationalism, then, becomes comprehensible in terms of this process. Writing of African nationalism, James S. Coleman has discussed the emergence of a "psychology of nationalism" that evolves with "an awareness of the existence or possibility of alternatives in the status quo, a state of mind produced by Western education."[11] Daniel Lerner, in his study of political development in the Middle East, has spoken of the emergence of a "mobile personality"—created by a high level of urbanization, literacy, and media participation—which has the capability to adapt to a changing environment.[12]

This basic argument has been elaborated upon considerably in recent years. Nationalism, the "ethos" of modernization, has

18   NATIONALISM AND ITS LEGACIES

come to be viewed by many as the ideology of the most modernized—i.e., of the new social classes spawned by the impact of the West.[13] It has also been defined as a psychic response to the more frightening consequences of modernization. As Lucian Pye has stated:

> This [the period in which modernization begins to take hold] is a . . . time of personal insecurity, for millions must make frightening adjustments in their personal perspectives on life. . . . In addition to suffering the pain and discomfort of being torn from the old and the known, they are confronted with the most basic of human issues, that of individual integrity and personal identity. For the old is, above all, that which friend and foe use without hesitation or qualification to define the uniqueness of the self, of the "we" which is the essence of identity in the human community; and the new is seen by friend and foe alike as the essence of that which is foreign.[14]

Nationalism is a response to the strain of modernization, providing "a symbolic outlet for emotional disturbances generated by social disequilibrium."[15]

Not only nationalism but also nationalist movements have come to be understood in terms of modernization. Those who participate in such movements are, almost by definition, modernized, articulating nationalist sentiment and joining nationalist movements as a result of that modernization. The development of a nationalist movement is seen as being concurrent with the spread of modernization, and nationalist movements become ground swells of modernity. This view does not imply that all participants in such movements are wholly modernized or necessarily nationalist in the Western understanding of the term. Nonetheless, it has generally been argued that those involved in nationalist movements have "a much greater awareness of a closeness of contact with 'national' compatriots as well as with the 'national' government."[16] The nationalist movement is the result of the gradual emergence of modern society, expanding as greater and greater numbers of

19

people are touched by modernization. Modernization, nationalism, and nationalist movements become, in other words, synonymous with one another.

The linkage of the nationalist movement to the widening impact of modernization is frequently utilized to explain major ideological differences over time within a single nationalist movement or between different movements. For example, surges of radical nationalism, of violent demands for immediate independence, are often discussed in terms of increasing numbers of less Westernized, less middle-class individuals in the movement. Such a surge seemed to occur in India in the 1920's after a series of organizational reforms within the Indian National Congress considerably widened participation in the movement.[17] Another surge occurred in the Gold Coast (now Ghana) when the middle-class party, the United Gold Coast Convention, was supplanted by a more militant Convention People's Party, dominated by "elementary-school leavers." Such individuals—"marked out by the limited system of secondary education through which they struggled to reach a minimum of qualifications"[18]—were linked into the modern economic and social system but only marginally so. Isolated from tradition yet unprepared for any effective role in modern society, the elementary-school leavers were seen as being even more impelled to nationalism than their middle-class counterparts.

Robert Nisbet, commenting on nationalism, has noted:

> Modern nationalism cannot be understood . . . apart from those rents and clefts in the traditional structure of human loyalties, caused by economic and social dislocation, which left widening masses of human beings in a kind of psychological vacuum.[19]

Most studies of nationalist movements suggest that a similar statement can be made about those movements. The emergence of such movements is seen as a consequence of the ever widening impact of modernization and the spread of nationalism. Nationalism, in essence, is the "passion" of modernization, and nationalist movements are the behavioral manifestations of that passion.

Non-Western Nationalism: A Reappraisal

The current understanding of nationalism in general and of non-Western nationalism in particular is both simple and persuasive. Several issues might be raised, however. That the emergence of nationalism is related to the spread of modernization seems incontestable. Yet, to view nationalism as simply an emotional response to the consequences of modernization—to the emergence of class interests, to the appearance of personal and social insecurity, and the like—tends to ignore the impact of Western ideas on nationalist elites and the elites' responses to such ideas. As we shall argue later, such responses are often inseparable from the nationalist movements that nationalist elites seek to build.

An even greater difficulty is engendered by the tendency to equate modernization, nationalism, and nationalist movements. If the growth of a nationalist movement is seen as the widening expression of nationalist sentiment resulting from the widening impact of modernization, the apparent lack of nationalist sentiment in underdeveloped states after independence (which has so often been decried) becomes something of a mystery. A paradox becomes apparent here. On the one hand, scholars of contemporary politics in the underdeveloped states see the persistence of parochialism and particularism as perhaps the dominant characteristic of these states in the post-independence period. On the other hand, the growth of nationalism, as seen in the nationalist movement, is especially emphasized in studies of the pre-independence period.

As was noted in the first chapter, modern social scientists tend to discuss social change in holistic terms. That is, societies are defined by a single characteristic social structure ("traditional," "modern"), and change is comprehended in terms of

21

sequences of such social structures. These structures may momentarily overlap, but ultimately one excludes the other.

That the modernization theory of nationalism makes such an assumption about social change is perhaps most visible in the various arguments that nationalism can be best understood in terms of stages. One scholar, for example, in a study of Congolese politics, has identified "five overlapping stages in the evolution of the nationalist movement":

1) Primary resistance movement
2) Messianic and syncretic sects
3) Urban riot and violence
4) Pre-political modern associations
5) Political parties[20]

In effect, each stage is symptomatic of a societal response to modernization and of the presence of particular types of social structures. Primary resistance movements are responses of a relatively stable traditional system to incursions by external forces. The collapse of traditional social structures sets the basis for intermittent responses, such as peasant *jacqueries*, messianic and syncretic cults, and urban riots and violence. The gradual crystallization of a new societal center and the expansion of that center—reflected in increasing numbers of Westernized elites and new "national" social, economic, and political institutions —produce the final stages of nationalism, the early political associations, and, ultimately, the nationalist political parties. Traditional, parochial institutions gradually give way to national institutions.

Such a picture of the development of nationalism not only overstates the modernizing consequences of social change but also ignores the differential impact of social change—even where it is modernizing—on the different societies that comprise the population of an area. Primary resistance movements, messianic cults, urban violence, and pre-political associations can occur simultaneously within one territory. The nationalist movement may not mark the beginnings of a national social sys-

NATIONALISM AND ITS LEGACIES

tem and a surge of national consciousness so much as an orchestration of protests—urban, rural, messianic, tribal, and nationalist.

The Sources of the Nationalist Movement

The sources of nationalism treated in the following sections are not "sources" in the sense that they represent preliminary stages to nationalism, as Crawford Young suggests. Given the differential impact of modernization, various protest movements seem to have occurred almost simultaneously, although one kind of protest may have tended to occur earlier in the colonial period (religious protest, for example). Nor are they "sources" because they have invariably forced their participants to begin to think in national terms. Rather, they are "sources" because they have provided social power that the nationalist elites can tap. The nationalist movement, as a result, has been not so much a cohesive mass movement as a collection of movements in a society segmented by region, community, kinship, and the pace of social change. In constructing a nationalist movement, nationalist elites have, in a sense, constructed a fiction, manipulating local protests and groups into concert with nationalist goals that are not necessarily widespread. In so doing, the nationalist elites have sought to legitimize both the demand for independence and their own position as leaders for independence.

URBAN POLITICS AND PROTEST

The first signs of political activity in Africa and Asia usually appeared in the cities and towns. Almost invariably these activities were organized and led by Westernized indigenous elites—the new middle class. A plethora of associations interlinked by common membership became characteristic of most urban societies.

Class interests served as the organizational impetus for much of the organizational activity. Spawned by conscious and unconscious governmental policies that swelled their numbers while at the same time curtailing their opportunities for employment and advancement, the Westernized elites gradually crystallized as a self-conscious class, concerned with their own particular class interests and identity.[21] The result was an incredibly diverse set of organizations and associations articulating those interests—traders' associations, civil servant groups, intellectual clubs, and overtly political associations, such as the Indian Association in Calcutta, the early Indian National Congress, the Tanganyikan African Association, and the Young Tunisians.[22] Most of these groups—whatever their formally stated purpose—served a variety of functions, often shifting from being intellectual discussion groups to organizing protests and back again. Their memberships generally overlapped. A study of the development of the nationalist movement in one district in Tanganyika, for example, notes that the activists in the local Tanganyikan African Association were also heavily involved in a traders' cooperative and in social-cultural clubs as well.[23] Similar patterns can be cited for India, the Congo, Morocco, Tunisia, and elsewhere.[24]

These middle-class associations also tended to be intermittent, organizing petitions and protest for a brief period and then lapsing into obscurity until a new set of issues developed (an event which often engendered a new set of groups). Some efforts were made to achieve wider economic and social reforms, but, in general, these groups remained largely class-oriented. Despite their concern for modern reforms, these groups remained essentially particularistic, responding to what were essentially local issues and problems. Any efforts to develop a geographically broader association or movement generally focused on issues of particular concern to the new middle classes, such as demands for enhanced civil service opportunities.

One common misconception of the Westernized elites is that they were isolated from traditional society, rootless as it were.[25] In reality, the Westernized elites continued to play important roles in their traditional communities. Commenting on this, one historian of nineteenth-century India has noted:

> An educated man continued to belong to a caste and a community, and hence he tended to belong to organizations of both kinds, one based on common kinship and religious persuasion and one based on common education and political persuasion.[26]

The strength of their traditional ties and their success in a nontraditional setting often combined to enable the Westernized elites, as atypical as they were, to remain effectively integrated into their traditional communities and to exert considerable influence in those communities.[27] As a result, these elites played a major role in organizing associations based on communal bonds—caste associations, tribal welfare associations, religious organizations, and the like.[28] To return to the Tanganyika example mentioned earlier, many of the elites active in the local branch of the Tanganyikan African Association also served as organizers of the Sukuma Union, a tribal association established "to encourage Sukuma to care for each other and to help each other with life's difficulties."[29]

These associations drew on tradition in terms of their base for membership, but they were not really traditional. Leadership was not necessarily supplied by those qualified by heredity but rather by those qualified by education. Such groups performed a variety of functions—promoting social reform within the community, acting as a mediator between disputing parties, encouraging and often actually sponsoring new educational facilities. These groups also served as the focal point for considerable protest activity. In India, caste associations organized within the lower castes often initiated protests against the religious and governmental discrimination practiced against their members.[30] Throughout Africa, especially in West Africa, similar protests occurred. These ethnic associations were, by and large, dominated by Westernized elites. They frequently served, however, to link diverse elements within one ethnic group more closely together.

The surge of social and political activity in the cities and towns was not restricted to the new middle class alone. The characteristically low wages and poor working conditions of the indigenous workers stimulated considerable trade union activity in certain places.[31] In large part, the impetus for such activity came from outside the working classes—either from local political elites or (especially in Africa) from European trade union bodies. The latter were particularly important in French Africa where the large French unions—the CGT, CFTC, and *Force Ouvrière*—established their own headquarters, to which individual unions were affiliated.

The unions, often restricted by law and unrecognized by employers, frequently resorted to strikes. Some widespread general strikes were attempted, most notably during the non-cooperation movements in India in 1920 and 1931, in Sudan in 1947, and in Ghana in 1950. In general, however, local strikes, in support of local objectives, were more characteristic of the trade union movement. Even where trade union activity was minimal, strikes often occurred. The tendency of the unskilled labor pool to far outstrip the employment opportunities—a situation exacerbated by an ever increasing migration to the cities—made lawless, and often violent, protest almost epidemic in these societies.

All of these groups—class or communal—tended to be sporadic and unstructured in organization and particularistic in orientation. The Westernized elites sought to focus and articulate diffuse feelings of discomfort and dissent among various social groups instead of soliciting new demands for which there was no ready-made base of popular support.[32] Many of the groups were interlinked by members, but there was seldom any attempt to unify the groups' efforts even within a particular urban setting. The different groups had different purposes, and different ones responded to varying problems and policies.

RURAL POLITICS AND PROTEST
Political mobilization was not a uniquely urban phenomenon. The rural areas also witnessed a considerable range of organizational and protest activities. The various movements

—peasant movements, nativistic and messianic cults, and cooperative movements—had diverse origins and support. Virtually all were limited in the scope of their objectives and their support. Particularistic politics and protest were even more symptomatic of the countryside than of the urban areas.

The impact of Western economy and ideas was felt in various ways in African and Asian societies. Western economic penetration into these areas provided for the development of a national economy and for its penetration into the local arena. The consequences were considerable; "North Atlantic capitalism," as Eric Wolf has called it, undermined the very basis of peasant society. The old village economy was brought to a slow death as the cash economy penetrated the village and destroyed its self-sufficiency. The peasant turned from subsistence farming to the cultivation of cash crops. In the process he converted his labor, his land, and his produce into commodities that were "subjected to the needs of a market which bore only a very indirect relation to the needs of the rural populations subjected to it."[33]

The expansion of the market economy also cut the customary bonds of peasant society. Traditionally, peasants strove to reduce risks and to improve their stability by sharing their resources within communal organizations and by relying on their ties with powerful patrons. Western capitalism tended to sever people from their social matrix and to transform them into economic actors, independent of prior social commitments to kin and neighbors.[34] The patron's role changed as well. Traditional patrons—tribal chiefs, landed noblemen, and the like—either gave way to the entrepreneur or adapted themselves to the new economy. In either case, their traditional links to the peasantry broke down. Supported by the colonial regime's power to enforce its own notions of law, the patron could ignore his traditional responsibilities to the local community. If he thus lost much of the social approval that he or his predecessor enjoyed, he gained an outside ally with the power to guarantee his local position.[35]

The nature of credit was also transformed. Although the

money lender was an actor in traditional village life, his ability to enforce usurious rates was generally sharply curtailed by village authorities and by custom. Land was often held communally, and money lenders had little legal recourse for the collection of debts. The colonial system often altered this drastically, allocating land to specific owners and supporting the money lender's claims. Such developments only exacerbated the already growing role for the money lenders. Even where legal changes were minimal, Western economic penetration favored money exchange at the expense of subsistence and barter economy, and it failed to provide reasonable credit facilities for the bulk of the people.[36] The peasant was increasingly driven to the money lender and forced to accept even the most usurious terms. A vicious circle developed—credit at usurious terms, hopeless indebtedness, alienation of land, decreasing bargaining power in marketing produce, and renewed demand for more credit. The farmer was reduced to a tenant, and the tenant to an agricultural laborer.

The peasant response to this situation was often violent rebellion, articulating the peasants' increasing sense of their vulnerability. More often than not, such rebellions were directed at the symbols of the peasants' condition, the landlords and money lenders, rather than at the state itself. The Saya San rebellion in Burma, the Moplah rebellion in southern India, the Tayug incident and the Sakdalist rebellion in the Philippines—these and others like them were transitory, violent, and limited in their goals. Where ideology played a role, it was less one of political nationalism than one of a millennial vision. As Eric R. Wolf has written:

> The peasant experience tends to be dualistic, in that he is caught between his understanding of how the world ought to be properly ordered and the realities of a mundane experience, beset by disorder. Against this disorder, the peasant has always set his dreams of deliverance, the vision of a Mahdi who would deliver the world from tyranny, of a son of Heaven who would truly embody the mandate of heaven. . . . Under conditions of modern dislocation, the disordered present is all too frequently experi-

NATIONALISM AND ITS LEGACIES

enced as world order reversed, and hence evil. . . . The true order is yet to come, whether through miraculous intervention, through rebellion, or both. Peasant anarchism and an apocalyptic vision of the world, together, provide the ideological fuel that drives the rebellious peasantry.[37]

Peasant protests were not always so short-lived. At times, local peasants' organizations developed and tried to ameliorate the peasant's situation politically. In India, the twentieth century witnessed the flourishing of *kisan sabhas* (cultivator associations). Protesting an increasingly complex land-tenure hierarchy, insecure land tenure, and an increasing number of ancillary taxes leveled by middle *rentiers*, the *kisan sabhas* achieved a considerable degree of organization and continuity in parts of India.[38] Such organizations seem to have crystallized as new patrons for their peasant members, who sought the *sabhas'* intervention against both landlords and government.

Regardless of the degree to which the peasants were organized, the peasant protests tended to be fairly restricted in scope, limited in both participants and territory affected. The conditions that spawned rural discontent were widespread. The discontent, however, remained relatively particularistic.

Another important aspect of peasant movements was their relation to religion. More often than not, they possessed a religious character, using religious symbols and rituals to mobilize support for social goals. The Saya San movement in Burma, for example, was led by a religious charlatan who infused messianic zeal into the movement. The Moplah rebellion in southern India in 1921 is another example of this mixture. Muslim peasants rose up, announcing the reestablishment of a caliphate kingdom while devoting most of their time and energy to assaulting Hindu money lenders.

A large number of religious movements, however, were concerned with the expressive needs of their participants rather than with any particular program of social change. These movements—messianic, syncretic, and revivalist—were a major associational form in the countryside. In Africa, messianic and syncretic cults—most of them amalgams of Christian millennialism and traditional custom—were the most prevalent. Such groups, called "Zionist" churches by Bengt Sundkler in his classic study of this phenomenon, usually developed around a particular prophet, stressed emotion and spontaneity in their rituals, were loosely organized, and emphasized prayer healing.[39]

Revivalism appears to have been characteristic of the religious movements in South Asia. Whether focused in the Hindu community—e.g., the Arya Samaj in northern India—or in the Muslim or other minority communities, the essential aim was the same: to strengthen the community, weakened by impure practices and degraded by colonialism, by returning the community to its religion as practiced in its (often legendary) golden age.[40]

Although religious movements assumed widely varying forms, what is important is that they were so prevalent. Religious movements provided the basis for widespread communication networks and, particularly where suppressed, sponsored a considerable number of protests. More important, despite a tendency on the part of scholars to see these movements as being restricted to an intermediate stage in the development of nationalism—representing "a period when no secular remedy to the frustrations engendered by the colonial situation seemed available"[41]—such movements appear to have had persisting impact. Religious movements not only created personal bonds between participants, which were often maintained even after the movement's fervor had died down, but also provided a vocabulary of expressive symbols. Such symbols were to become increasingly important as nationalist elites began to mobilize the countryside.

Not all associational efforts in the countryside focused on protests. In response to their economic situation, peasants sometimes attempted to develop producer cooperatives which sought to gain a greater role in the market system for the producer by eliminating the middlemen.[42]

Cooperative development appears to be as old as colonization itself. The first such society in East Africa was organized in 1908 by Western settlers; cooperatives in South Asia appeared even earlier. The cooperative efforts received some government encouragement, not necessarily for the reason their organizers stressed (protection of producer interests), but because colonial governments often felt that coops were the most efficient and effective way to bring the indigenous producer into the mainstream of the cash economy.

Although cooperative development has not been scrutinized in any great detail, it does appear that the middle-class elites so active in associational organizations were often initiators of cooperative movements. In Gambia, the senior Gambian nationalist, Pa Small, was the major impetus for the cooperative movement.[43] Maguire's study of Tanzania reveals that the leader of the Tanganyikan African Association (TAA) and the tribal association was the leading organizer of the producer cooperatives as well. One cooperative organizer, with a core group of assistants, moved into a rural area and gradually expanded his contacts with village elders and young men's societies.[44]

By and large, however, cooperative societies had only limited success. Colonial governments distrusted their potentially political role, and traditional elites were often openly hostile to them. Perhaps more important, the cooperatives were hampered by inadequate capital and by a simple institutional inability to reach the level where the need was greatest—the tenant cultivator, deeply in debt, who had neither securities to pledge for loans nor enough savings to repay what he did manage to borrow.

Where they were successful, however, cooperatives provided a considerable degree of associational infrastructure. As Maguire has noted, "in terms of statistics alone, the cooperatives by 1954 had something like ten times the number of members (approximately 30,000) of either the TAA or the Sukuma Union (approximately 3,000 each)."[45] The cooperatives established links that offered Westernized elites direct access to the countryside.

31

The basis for the largest part of social activity in Africa and Asia continued to be traditional social structures. Traditional societies were usually complex interweavings of kinship, rank, mutual dependence, and custom. More often than not, these societies were vertically organized. Traditional notables were linked vertically to socially inferior groups through ties of deference and self-interest, a set of mutual dependencies that is generally discussed in terms of patron-client relationships.[46] Highly localized, these relationships, in effect, defined the social universe for their participants.

Even where the Western impact had begun to be felt, patron-client relationships often persisted. As a result of the more complex economic and political structure of the colonial society, the Western impact often tended to narrow the scope of exchange between patron and client and to increase radically the importance of external resources for local patronage (thereby converting the local patron into a broker between the village and the larger system). In some cases, however, the traditional patrons successfully utilized new resources of the colonial society and accentuated their role. Lemarchand, for example, has reported:

> In the national context of Nigeria, the "traditionally august figures" of the Northern Region played the role of brokers or middlemen; poised between the national and regional cultures and communities, they became the manipulators of first- and second-order resources—i.e., of patronage offices, loans, scholarships and contracts on one hand, and of contracts and connections on the other. Similar roles have been played with greater or lesser degrees of success by the *ganwa* in Burundi, the *sheikhs* in Senegal, the *hassan* and *zawya* in Mauretania, the *saza* chiefs in Buganda and some traditional chiefs in the Ivory Coast, Ghana, Niger, and Upper Volta.[47]

Even where social change worked to undermine the power of the patron, such change was not always accompanied by a decline in the patron's social power. Traditional patrons often retained their clientele network despite their supplantation by newer, better connected patrons. Certain peasants persisted in their links to their traditional patrons, either out of deference or out of the mistaken belief that such men really did possess influence.

Not all traditional social structures, in other words, crumbled in the face of Western influences. Even where traditional patterns of authority were disrupted, those who had wielded authority (and lost it to the colonial power, for example) often retained their position in the social matrix.

Linkage Politics: The Nationalist Movement Achieved

The development of a widespread nationalist movement is, in part, the consequence of fundamental organizational changes occurring among the nationalist elites. These changes—variously summarized as the emergence of mass parties, or of a national party center, or of a mobilizational nationalist party—generally work to formalize relationships between the various levels within the nationalist elite (local, regional, and national) and to facilitate linkages between those elites and local movements and social groups.

The changes that took place in the Indian National Congress between 1919 and 1921 illustrate this linkage process. In the early part (1885-1920) of the Indian National Congress's history, the party was really an amalgam of middle-class elites located in the principal cities of India. Throughout this period, Congress expansion was principally an expansion into urban India. Local and provincial organizations functioned almost autonomously and involved relatively small numbers of individuals. The "national" Congress was symbolized by a few leaders of national stature and by yearly all-India gatherings. The Congress gradually developed an organizational infrastructure as it became involved in negotiating for reforms in colonial rule and as Congress elites involved themselves in a widening sphere of social, economic, and political activities.[48] To some degree, the moderate-extremist division that characterized internal Congress politics during this period facilitated organizational growth because competing factions sought to expand their influence among Congress sympathizers.[49]

The process of organizational development did not, however, achieve its full momentum until the early 1920's when Mohandas K. Gandhi assumed leadership.[50] Almost immediately a variety of organizational changes were instituted. An active, day-to-day party executive, the Working Committee, was formed, as were ongoing executive committees at the provincial and local levels. Financial resources were expanded; and the emergence of full-time party organizers was encouraged. Perhaps most important, the 1920 Congress Constitution laid down that the Provincial Congresses should not follow British administrative divisions (as they had up until that time) but rather the linguistic divisions within India. Accordingly, the existing provincial units were reorganized into twenty-one linguistically homogeneous jurisdictions.

The reforms resulted in a more formally organized Congress. Stable communication links were established between the newly developed party center and party branches, and the number of professional party workers grew at all levels of the party. In addition, these reforms enhanced the ability of the Congress elites to penetrate into local politics. Congress deliberations were conducted in local languages. Party professionals were able to become more actively involved in local groups and protests.

The Indian case was not especially unique. In his study of the Ivory Coast, Zolberg has traced a similar pattern of organizational development for the *Parti Démocratique de Côte d'Ivoire* (PDCI). In 1947, an attempt was made to transform the coalition-like PDCI into a monolithic mass organization.[51] The executive committee was reorganized, a cadre school was established to train party organizers, and, on paper, the party was transformed into a vertically organized, cell-based mass organization.[52] The PDCI and other parties[53] were formed by or fell under the sway of organizational elites concerned with

34

organized to gain more authority = failure
ex-PDCI

gaining a mass following, and they were structured or restructured to facilitate linkages between themselves and other social
groups. Party professionals actively canvassed for support and
often embroiled themselves in local protests to engender such
support.

While mass-oriented nationalist parties had a considerable
advantage vis-à-vis other parties and often gained considerable
followings, they were usually far from massive. In the 1952 elections in the Ivory Coast, the PDCI polled only about 33 percent
of those eligible to vote. In Ghana in 1951, the Convention
People's Party (CPP) gained the support of about 30 percent
of those eligible to vote.[54] Nor were other parties more successful in the early period of their mass-oriented activities. The
Indian National Congress, for example, was not able to demon-
strate truly massive support until just prior to independence.

Nor did the emergence of mass-oriented nationalist organizations mean the emergence of highly organized nationalist
parties. One study of the mass-oriented West African nationalist
parties has shown that they were actually very rudimentary in
organization.[55]

> The new wave [of nationalists] accomplished its initial aim
> with very meager means. They used bicycles, a few trucks,
> or very occasionally an automobile. They sometimes had
> some private funds, but relied mainly upon a small band
> of dedicated men. The organizations they created were at
> first very limited: some form of executive compound of the
> co-founders, a larger group of correspondents with contacts
> among various voluntary associations, mainly in the capital
> and a few key towns in the hinterland, and among various
> ethnic groups. The organizations were centered in the capi-
> tal and extended to a handful of branches in the hinter-
> land.[56]

center = resources
inability to spread because lack of resources

What emerged, in fact, was a political phenomenon totally
different from what we call an organized party: it was a highly
segmented movement with the various segments linked to one
another by nationalist elites and the nationalist party organization. The *Bloc Démocratique Sénégalais*, the first mass-oriented

party in Senegal, was, in theory, modeled after the French Socialist Party (SFIO) but, in reality, it emerged as a very segmented party. The branches of the party were generally dominated by local notables, and through them the party emerged as a haphazard collage of ethnic groups and political-kinship factions called clans. Zolberg, discussing one urban branch of the PDCI (theoretically patterned after the Communist party model), has noted that its 20,000 members were divided among more than 100 ethnic subcommittees.[57]

The emergence of this kind of organization is, perhaps, best understood by noting the relationship between the initial organizational changes and the nationalist elites. Such changes mark the real beginnings of institutionalization for a party.[58] The organization begins to develop its own set of roles,[59] its own elite selection process (elite status is, in part, conferred on the basis of organizational skill, success in communicating party ideology, and occupancy of party offices), its own decision-making process, and its own unique internal groups (usually factions based on personal, organizational, and ideological conflicts). On paper, at least, the party is a highly disciplined, highly autonomous entity.

As just noted, however, these changes mark only the beginnings of an institutionalization process, and the party possesses far less autonomy in reality than it does in theory.[60] This is particularly visible in terms of party roles. Elite status is not so much endowed by the party (party offices, for example) as it is confirmed by the party. Individuals become dominant figures at the various levels of the newly organized or reorganized party because of their existing elite status in other social, political, and economic groups, and they rise in the party on the basis of their ability to utilize those connections to their advantage. Their elite status in the party, in turn, buttresses their status in the other groups.

This elite linkage process is visible in virtually all nationalist movements. Patrice Lumumba, the Congolese nationalist leader, is but one example. Shortly after his arrival in Stanleyville in 1951, Lumumba joined the leading intellectual club,

36

the *Association des Evolves de Stanleyville*. That same year he was appointed Secretary-General of the *Association des Postiers de la Province Orientale*. By 1953, Lumumba was a full-fledged member of no less than *seven* associations. By 1955, he was chairman of both the *Association des Evolves* and the *Association du Personnel Indigène de la Colonie* of Stanleyville, an indigenous labor organization restricted to African civil servants. In 1956, he founded the *Amicale Libérale de Stanleyville*. Two years later he became one of the founders of the *Mouvement National Congolais*, which became the first Congo-wide nationalist organization.[61] Similar biographies can be cited for most of the major nationalist leaders. More important, however, such biographies can be compiled for most of the lower-echelon party elites as well. Paul Bomani, one of the activists noted by Maguire in his Sukuma district study, was in many ways typical. Bomani was a leader of the Mwanza African Traders Cooperative Society, an organizer of producer cooperatives in the area, and a leader of the provincial cooperative movement.[62] In 1951, Bomani became president of the Sukuma Union, the Sukuma tribal association, and in 1952, president of the Lake Province Tanganyikan African Association.[63] Extensive studies of local political elites reveal this pattern repeatedly.[64]

The nationalist parties do not supplant the local associations and movements so much as they link to them via the nationalist elites. In effect, the personal ambition of the "national" nationalist elites, their nationalism, and their desire to build a widespread movement dovetail, and a "nationalist movement" —a highly segmented, interlinked set of local protests and groups—appears. In Tanganyika, the nationalist elites in the TAA (which was reorganized and renamed the Tanganyikan African National Union—TANU—in 1954) were active in a variety of local protests throughout the territory—strikes in one area, protests against government restrictions on cooperatives in another, protests against legislation restricting land use in yet other areas. In the area studied by Maguire, virtually all of these protests funneled into a continuous outbreak of civil disobedience in 1958.[65] In much of the area, TANU was successfully able to interlink the protests with its own demands: Julius Nyerere, the national TANU leader, toured the area in a successful membership campaign, and a local TANU leader emerged as the symbolic leader and, eventually, martyr of the protests. Elsewhere, TANU often orchestrated more limited numbers of groups and protests. In West Lake Province, for example, the nationalist movement was an interlinkage of tribal groups and coffee growers' cooperatives.[66]

In Guinea, the mass component and the leadership of the nationalist movement, led by the *Parti Démocratique de Guinée* (PDG), were supplied by the industrial labor force. Sekou Touré, the PDG leader who had been thrown into the limelight by his trade union leadership, welded together a nationalist movement on a militant trade union base. In Soudan (now Mali), the *Union Soudanaise* was an interlinkage between trade unions, the Niger River trading community and their clients, and traditional elites such as the ruling Haidara family of Timbuktu.[67] In Algeria, the *Front de Libération Nationale* linked urban labor insurrections, peasant revolts, and reformist Islam networks.[68]

In general, nationalist elites formed the nexus for the movement as a whole, and through their own social networks they melded together a variety of particularistic protests and groups. As becomes obvious from the examples, the movements varied widely in the kind of groups and protests interlinked. The same was generally true within a particular movement, as the Tanganyikan example illustrates. A nationalist movement can vary widely in character in different areas of a country. During Gandhi's first Noncooperation Movement in India in 1920-1921, the movement in Punjab was an amalgam of two religious revivalist movements—one, Islam; one, Sikh—and a much smaller genuinely nationalist urban protest group.[69] In the United Provinces, in contrast, the movement was more a meld of urban nationalist protest and localized peasant movements.

As a result of this linkage process, different mass-oriented nationalist organizations within the same area produced nationalist movements of widely different character. In Sierra

NATIONALISM AND ITS LEGACIES

Leone, the different parties not only drew on different ethnic groups but on different kinds of social groupings as well. The Sierra Leone People's Party was closely linked to a wide variety of neotraditional tribal associations.[70] The more radical nationalist United Progressive Party and People's National Party were linked to more lawless kinds of economic and political protest. The United Progressive Party, for instance, obtained the main body of its members during the tax riots in 1955-1956 when the party's leader freely placed his legal skills at the service of thousands of tax rioters.[71]

A Note on Nationalism As a Political Concept

The varying character of nationalist movements raises the question of the ultimate source of the differences. Neither the nationalist elites' decision to try to build a nationalist movement nor the extent of participation in the movement is an historical inevitability. Ceylon is only one example where the nationalist movement remained largely an elite pastime.[72] More often than not, the differences between nationalist movements reflect conscious decisions on the part of nationalist elites that, first, their demands can only be resolved by immediate, total independence and, second, that only certain allies are legitimate in that drive for independence.

As we have previously stated, the modern view of nationalism is that it is a set of beliefs engendered by certain kinds of social change. Modern studies of nationalism, as a result, have sought to determine the roots of the sentiment called nationalism. Those roots become all-important. The programs of any particular nationalism are, as one scholar has noted, "epiphenomena," for such programs reflect only the particular circumstances of history.[73]

If, in contrast, it is argued—and it is here—that nationalism and nationalist movements are not synonymous, that nationalist movements are in fact the conscious constructions of the nationalist elites, it can also be argued that such movements

39

reflect the purposes and goals—both shared and unshared—of their constructors. Since a nationalist movement is far from a simple accretion to the sentiment known as nationalism, an understanding of the nature of the community that the nationalist elites are seeking is essential to understanding the nationalist movement they seek to build. In part, the question of community is answered by history and sociology. The question "Who are we?" is partially answered in terms of common historical experiences and of common ethnic bonds. But, the question "Who are we?" is also answerable in political terms—in decisions about the nature of the political order to be sought and the proper strategies and tactics to be used. Nationalist leaders do not simply mouth the rantings of modern times. They articulate what they perceive to be a proper political order and make conscious choices on that basis.

This is not to suggest that the nationalist elites are philosophers or that explicit ideologies have general relevance throughout a nationalist movement. Rather, what is being suggested is that the aspirations of certain elites, whatever the sources of those aspirations—socialization, ideology, "strain," economic interest, insecurity—have relevance in the construction of a nationalist movement in terms of what are viewed as legitimate tactics and goals and who are viewed as legitimate allies.[74] They also have relevance in defining the nature of some incipient or overt divisions among the nationalist elites.

Conclusion

Earlier in this chapter a paradox was raised: the contrast between scholars of contemporary politics in the underdeveloped states who emphasize the persistence of parochialism and those students of the nationalist period who see the demise of such parochialism as the dominant characteristic of that era. The former view becomes almost incomprehensible in the face of the latter. One effort to overcome this paradox has been to focus on the weakness, until recently unnoticed, of the nationalist organizations. The weakness continues, it is argued, after independence until the point is reached where the forces of modernization can no longer be managed. Stability breaks down, and traditionalism becomes resurgent in the vacuum created by the collapse of the modernizing elements of society.

Such a characterization contains truth. Yet, it glosses over the nature of the nationalist movement itself. A segmented, contradictory collection of nationalism and particularism, the nationalist movement represents only a tenuous unity of protest. The problem after independence is less resurgent traditionalism than the inability of political elites to find new sources of unity.

NOTES

1. See, in particular, Carleton Hayes, *Nationalism: A Religion* (New York: Macmillan, 1960); and Hans Kohn, *The Age of Nationalism: The First Era of Global History* (New York: Harper and Row, 1962).

2. This does not mean that the emotional element was not stressed. Hans Kohn, for example, writes of nationalism being "more than anything else, a state of mind." See Kohn, *Nationalism: Its Meaning and History* (Princeton: Van Nostrand, 1965), p. 9.

3. Karl W. Deutsch, *Nationalism and Social Communication* (New York and Cambridge: M.I.T. and John Wiley and Sons, 1953), p. 16.

4. This approach is most associated with the writings of Karl Deutsch.

5. *Ibid.*, p. 97.

6. *Ibid.*, chapter 4.

7. *Ibid.*, chapter 8.

8. See, for example, Kohn, *Nationalism*, p. 10.

9. Rupert Emerson, *From Empire to Nation* (Boston: Beacon Press, 1960), p. 188.

10. Karl W. Deutsch, "Social Mobilization and Political Development," *American Political Science Review*, LV, 3 (1961), 494.

11. James S. Coleman, "Nationalism in Tropical Africa," *American Political Science Review*, XLVIII, 2 (1954), 404-426.

12. Daniel Lerner, *The Passing of Traditional Society* (New York: Free Press, 1958), especially pp. 43-75.

13. Martin Kilson, Jr., "Nationalism and Social Classes in British West Africa," *Journal of Politics*, XX, 2 (1958), 368-409.

14. Lucian Pye, *Politics, Personality, and Nation Building* (New Haven: Yale University Press, 1962), p. 4.

15. Clifford Geertz, "Ideology as a Cultural System," in David E. Apter, ed., *Ideology and Discontent* (New York: Free Press, 1964), p. 54.

16. Coleman, p. 404.

17. Gopal Krishna, "The Development of the Indian National Congress as a Mass Organization," *Journal of Asian Studies* XXV, 3 (1966), 413-430, discusses these reforms and their impact in detail.

18. Dennis Austin, *Politics in Ghana, 1946-1960* (London: Oxford University Press, 1970), pp. 13-14.

19. Robert Nisbet, *Community and Power* (New York: Oxford University Press, 1962), p. 164.

20. Crawford Young, *Politics in the Congo* (Princeton: Princeton University Press, 1965), p. 281.

21. Kilson, p. 385. An excellent study of this contradiction of policy on the part of the colonial government can be found in Briton Martin, Jr., *New India, 1885* (Berkeley and Los Angeles: University of California Press, 1969).

22. For an excellent introduction to associational activities in Africa, see Thomas Hodgkin, *Nationalism in Colonial Africa* (New York: New York University Press, 1957), pp. 84-92.

23. G. Andrew Maguire, *Toward 'Uhuru' in Tanzania* (Cambridge, Eng.: Cambridge University Press, 1969), pp. 63-75.

24. See the various country studies cited in this chapter.

25. This is the basis for the whole nationalism-as-a-response-to-insecurity argument noted earlier.

26. Anil Seal, *The Emergence of Indian Nationalism* (Cambridge, Eng.: Cambridge University Press, 1968), pp. 15-16.

27. Georges Balandier, *The Sociology of Black Africa* (New York: Frederick A. Praeger, 1970), p. 388.

28. For an excellent study of the role of these elites in building caste associations in India, see Lloyd I. Rudolph and Susanne Hoeber Rudolph, *The Modernity of Tradition* (Chicago: University of Chicago Press, 1967), Part I. A bibliographical footnote on studies of these associations can be found on pp. 62-63.

29. Maguire, pp. 75-76.

30. Rudolph and Rudolph, pp. 36-64.

31. See, for example, W. M. Warren, "Urban Real Wages and the Nigerian Trade Union Movement, 1939-60," *Economic Development and Cultural Change*, XV, 1 (1966), 21-36.

32. Richard Sisson, *The Congress Party in Rajasthan* (Berkeley and Los Angeles: University of California Press, 1972), p. 48.

33. Eric R. Wolf, "On Peasant Rebellions," *International Social Science Journal*, XXI, 2 (1969), 287.

34. Eric R. Wolf, *Peasant Wars of the Twentieth Century* (New York: Harper and Row, 1969), p. 279.

35. James C. Scott, "Patron-Client Politics and Political Change in Southeast Asia," *American Political Science Review*, LXVI, 1 (1972), 108.

36. Erich H. Jacoby, *Agrarian Unrest in Southeast Asia* (New York: Columbia University Press, 1949), p. 21.

37. Wolf, *Peasant Wars*, p. 295.

38. See Walter Hauser, *Agrarian Movements in India* (forthcoming) for an excellent survey of the large number of activities carried on by these organizations.

39. Bengt Sundkler, *Bantu Prophets in South Africa*, 2nd ed. (New York: Oxford University Press, 1961). For studies of specific movements, see Robert C. Mitchell, "Religious Protest and Social Change: The Origins of the Aladura Movement in Western Nigeria," in Robert I. Rotberg and Ali A. Mazrui, eds., *Protest and Power in Black Africa* (New York: Oxford University Press, 1970); James W. Fernandez "The Affirmation of Things Past: Alar Ayong and Bwiti as Movements of Protest in Central and Northern Gabon," in *ibid.*; Thomas Hodgkin, *Nationalism and Colonial Africa* (London: Oxford University Press, 1956); George Shepperson, "Ethiopianism and African Nationalism," *Phylon*, XIV (March 1953), 9-19, and "The Politics of African Church Separatist Movements in British Central Africa, 1892-1916," *Africa*, XXIV (July 1954), 233-237; and Michael Banton, "African Prophets," *Race*, V, 2 (October 1963), 42-55.

40. For a study of the Arya Samaj, see Kenneth Jones, "The Arya Samaj in Punjab, 1880-1902" (Ph.D. dissertation, University of California, Berkeley, 1965). For material on Muslim revivalism in South Asia, see Aziz Ahmad, *Islamic Modernism in India and Pakistan* (London: Oxford University Press, 1967).

41. Young, p. 254.

42. For one study of cooperative societies that has a broader theoretical scope than its title implies, see Arthur Dobrin, *The Role of Agrarian Cooperatives in the Development of Kenya*, Studies in Comparative International Development, V, 1969-1970, No. 6.

43. S. A. S. Nyang, "Problems of Gambian Cooperatives" (M.A. thesis, University of Virginia, 1971), pp. 14-26.

44. Maguire, pp. 109-110.

45. *Ibid.*, p. 109.

46. The patron-client relationship may be defined as a special case of dyadic (two-person) ties involving a largely instrumental friendship in which an individual of higher socioeconomic status (patron) uses his own influence and resources to provide protection or benefits, or both, for a person of lower status (client) who, for his part, reciprocates by offering general support and assistance, including personal services, to the patron. On such relationships see, especially, George M. Foster, "The Dyadic Contract in Tzintzuntzan: Patron-Client Relationship," *American Anthropologist*, LXV (1963), 1280-1294; Eric Wolf, "Kinship, Friendship, and Patron-Client Relations," in Michael Banton, ed., *The Social Anthropology of Complex Societies*, Association of Applied Social Anthropology Monograph #4 (London: Tavistock Publications, 1966), pp. 1-22; John Duncan Powell, "Peasant Society and Clientelist Politics," *American Political Science Review*, LXIV, 2 (1970), 411-425; René

Lemarchand, "Political Clientelism and Ethnicity in Tropical Africa: Competing Solidarities in Nation-Building," *American Political Science Review*, LXVI, 1 (1972), 68-90; and Scott.

47. Lemarchand, p. 80.

48. For an excellent study of this role-expansion on the part of Congress elites, see Charles Heimsath, *Indian Nationalism and Hindu Social Reform* (Princeton: Princeton University Press, 1964).

49. On these divisions, see Daniel Argov, *Moderates and Extremists in the Nationalist Movement* (Bombay: Asia Publishing House, 1967).

50. The following discussion is drawn, in large part, from Krishna.

51. Aristide Zolberg, *One-Party Government in the Ivory Coast* (Princeton: Princeton University Press, 1964), p. 113.

52. *Ibid.*, p. 116.

53. For material on other mass-oriented parties, see, for example, David E. Apter, *Ghana in Transition* (New York: Atheneum, 1963); Lars Rudebeck, *Party and People: A Study of Political Change in Tunisia* (New York: Frederick A. Praeger, 1968); Richard L. Sklar, *Nigerian Political Parties* (Princeton: Princeton University Press, 1963); and John Cady, *A History of Modern Burma* (Ithaca: Cornell University Press, 1958).

54. Aristide Zolberg, *Creating Political Order: The Party-States of West Africa* (Chicago: Rand, McNally and Co., 1966), p. 15.

55. *Ibid.*, pp. 19-36.

56. *Ibid.*, p. 13.

57. Zolberg, *One-Party Government in the Ivory Coast*, p. 116.

58. On the concept of institutionalization, see Chapter 1, footnote 2.

59. "Role" may be defined as a pattern of expected behavior for individuals holding particular positions in a system.

60. Organizational "autonomy" is defined as the degree to which an organization has its own roles, norms, values, and interests, distinguishable from those of any other group or institution. For a discussion of this concept, see Huntington, pp. 20-22.

61. René Lemarchand, "Patrice Lumumba," in W. A. E. Skurnik, ed., *African Political Thought: Lumumba, Nkrumah, and Touré*, Graduate School of International Studies Monograph, Volume 5, Numbers 3 and 4, 1967-1968 (Denver, Col.: University of Denver, 1968).

62. Maguire, pp. 83, 86-88.

63. *Ibid.*, p. 136.

64. See, for example, Paul Brass, *Factional Politics in an Indian State* (Berkeley and Los Angeles: University of California Press, 1965); Donald B. Rosenthal, *The Limited Elite* (Chicago: University of Chicago Press, 1970); and R. William Liddle, *Ethnicity, Party, and National Integration: An Indonesian Case Study* (New Haven: Yale University Press, 1970).

65. Maguire, pp. 196-242.

66. Göran Hýden, *Political Development in Rural Tanzania* (Nairobi: East Africa Publishing House, 1969), pp. 125-140.

67. *Ibid.*, p. 31; and Aristide Zolberg, "Political Revival in Mali," *Africa Report*, 10, 7 (1965), 18.

68. On Algeria, see William B. Quandt, *Revolution and Political Leadership: Algeria, 1954-1968* (Cambridge, Mass.: M.I.T. Press, 1969).

69. See Gerald A. Heeger, "The Politics of Integration: Community, Party, and Integration in Punjab" (Ph.D. dissertation, University of Chicago, 1971), pp. 16-49.

70. Martin Kilson, *Political Change in a West African State* (Cambridge, Mass.: Harvard University Press, 1966), pp. 259-265.

71. *Ibid.*, p. 237.

72. See W. Howard Wriggins, *Ceylon: Dilemmas of a New Nation* (Princeton: Princeton University Press, 1960); and Calvin A. Woodward, *The Growth of the Party System in Ceylon* (Providence: Brown University Press, 1969).

73. Leonard Binder, *The Ideological Revolution in the Middle East* (New York: John Wiley and Sons, 1964), p. 109.

74. For an argument that economic interest is the basis of nationalism, see Kilson, "Nationalism and Social Classes"; for arguments on the role of "strain" and "insecurity," see Geertz; Pye; and Charles F. Andrain, "The Political Thought of Sekou Touré," in Skurnik, ed., pp. 129-136.

3

The Search for Political Stability

I ndependence presents a crisis of management for the leaders of the nationalist movement. They must not only formulate new goals for themselves and the new state but also mobilize the resources to attain those goals. Because preferences differ, the elites must effect some degree of political consolidation, both between elites themselves and between elites and nonelites. Political consolidation appears to have three requisites: cohesion between the various political elites; mass compliance to shared elite preferences; and, because compliance is rarely sufficient to attain developmental goals, popular support.

All of these requisites are very much absent at independence. At that time the heightened political activity of the nationalist period serves to produce what is, at best, a collage of disparate elites and their followings. In the sense that one can speak of a center and a periphery of a society, a center of the nationalist movement is almost nonexistent.[1] The goals and symbols articulated by the movement are as diverse as the movement itself.

The problems of political consolidation seemed almost naturally to lead political scientists first studying them to emphasize ideology, charisma, and political parties as the means for achieving that consolidation. We say "almost naturally" not only because the leaders of these states were themselves emphasizing ideology, political parties, and their own personal qualities but also because such phenomena were, in a sense, the most visible to the Western eye. Hence, charismatic leadership was seen as providing a common focal point for a multitude of societies that, at first glance at least, seemed to have no other connection with one another. The charisma of Nkrumah, Sukarno, Nehru, Houphouet-Boigny, in effect, consolidated the state by

Charisma

> serving as a source of norms which became a standard for followers; serving as a symbol which helps disparate groups in the territorial society acquire a sense of identity with one another; serving as a focus for political integration, by appearing as the central figure of authority within the new institutional framework; and, finally, serving as a living symbol of the new territorial community, encouraging individuals to transcend traditional ethnic group affiliations.[2]

Ideology was seen as providing a common conceptual map to both elites and masses.[3] By providing new solidarity groupings in the form of party branches, political parties, particularly those associated with charismatic leaders and well-developed ideologies, were seen as the means by which both mass compliance and support could be achieved.

Recent events have demonstrated that all of these conceptualizations are limited in their ability to communicate the problems involved in achieving political consolidation. Charisma, where it existed, proved short-lived; and its effectiveness in securing any degree of solidarity, as David Apter has noted in his revised study of Ghana, is highly questionable.[4] Ideology is similarly limited. As Henry Bienen has stated:

> It is false to assume that explicit ideologies . . . have any general relevance; they may be espoused by only a select few who themselves may be removed from the center of power within the party. The aspirations of certain elites to transform their societies through a single party which penetrates all communities and social structures and mobilizes society's resources may or may not be significant.[5]

Nor has the study of political parties in underdeveloped societies been successful in clarifying the process of political consolidation. Early studies frequently mistook the organizational aspirations of the political elites for reality and posited a cohesion that simply was not there.[6] Later studies, while more cognizant of reality, continued to overemphasize the role of party in the consolidation process.

In brief, charisma, ideology, and political parties are all too simple to encompass the problem of political consolidation in its full scope. While factionalism among the political elites quickly asserted itself as a frequent cause of instability in the underdeveloped states and elicited much comment, it had little impact on theory. Most of the analyses tended to gloss over the diversity of the elites and their potential, if not actual, fragmentation.

At best, political consolidation was seen as preeminently a problem of elite-mass integration. Here, too, the formulations were simplistic. Elite-mass consolidation was viewed as being comprehensible in terms of but a single successful linkage between center and periphery—charisma, the party, etc. To put this in another way, where such linkages were seen to exist, the relationships they were seen as establishing were given more coherence than they possessed in reality. The actual multiplicity of such links and their possible contradiction were either obscured or ignored altogether. The more recent, revisionist studies of the supposedly monolithic political parties are not to be exempted from this criticism. While these studies point to the existence of considerably less cohesion between center and periphery than originally theorized, they, too, focus on political consolidation in terms of a single mechanism—in this case, the development of a political party machine.[7]

It will be argued here that the segmentary character of the new political systems limits the capability of any regime —regardless of type, regardless of whatever authoritarian aspirations a particular set of ruling elites may have—to consolidate that political system. As stated previously, the political process in underdeveloped states is defined by elite efforts to coalesce with one another in order to construct national institutions in the political center and in order to enlist societal support for those institutions. The institutions which emerge from this process are characterized by coalitions of semi-autonomous elites and groups at the local, regional, and national levels.

The coming of political independence radically alters the context in which politics is conducted. Independence provides—both through the inheritance of political institutions established during the colonial period and through the new leaders' conscious construction—for the emergence, at least in theory, of a political center in the form of central government and political institutions. Strategic political roles within those institutions are defined, as are the rules for performing those roles.

The segmentation characteristic of the nationalist movement alters in this context. While the segments do not disappear, political conflict within the system becomes focused on gaining access to and control of the various strategic political roles within the new political center. Access and control secure participation in the making of policy and, perhaps more important, in the distribution of the tangible and intangible benefits of government. Control of senior government and political positions brings with it control over the channels of decision-making; over the allocation of scarce resources such as business licenses, government loans, and jobs; and over the very degree to which the government will be responsive to particular groups and their demands. From being "orchestrations of protest," nationalist movements are changed into national arenas in which elites and groups compete for dominance and, through that dominance, for control of the government.

The very degree of segmentation of underdeveloped societies, however, limits the resources of any one group or set of elites to dominate the new political system. The search for dominance, then, serves as an impetus for coalition as the various elites and groups coalesce to create political units actually capable of securing dominance.

In the underdeveloped societies, government and the powers of government are the primary resources for creating and maintaining political organization. That is to say, once control over government is achieved, public power is utilized for what are, in effect, private purposes. The coalition of ruling elites is expanded at the expense of competing groups. Political institutions in underdeveloped systems are less actual organizations than they are masks for momentary coalitions. Control of the authority and resources of government—limited as they may be—provides the means by which institutions can be developed. By selective use of coercion, spoils, and patronage as well as of the government's limited legitimacy, institutions (such as a political party) and the coalitions that control them are built and expanded, attracting the support and participation of other groups and elites.

This intertwinement of government and other political institutions, such as political parties, must be underscored. According to prevailing scholarly conceptions, political parties are discrete organizational entities, apart from governmental institutions.[8] Such conceptions ignore the organizational poverty of political institutions in the underdeveloped states. Few organizations possess the resources to sustain themselves, and what appears to be an organization may in fact be little more than a small congeries of elites, in the case of an opposition political party, for example. Government parties, in contrast, are usually just that, organized through the use of governmental authority and apparatus. Deprived of that authority and apparatus, such a party is, similarly, likely to become a congeries of elites.

The almost classic distinctions between those states with parties and those without, between those ruled by political elites and those ruled by military or bureaucratic elites, may well be overstated. The various types of regimes may differ in terms of the institutional context in which elites organize the coalitional networks after they assume power: for example, party regimes may attempt to focus such networks within a party hierarchy; bureaucratic regimes, within a civil service hierarchy, etc.[9] However, all regimes in their search for consolidation and stability are inevitably led to a process of coalition and alliance.

Organizing the Political Center

Political consolidation is, in the first instance, focused around the development of sufficient cohesion among elites so that government can be organized. Such coalitions of elites tend to be highly tentative. Although the various elites and their followings coalesce to form more effective political units, they persist in holding a certain subidentity within the new structure.

Such cohesion may be simply the result of the individual elites' concern for short-run material gain. The governmental structures that comprise the new political center, which were both inherited from the colonial period and created at independence, serve as allocation centers, generating jobs, loans, economic aid, favorable administration of laws, and so forth. The mere availability of such potential may attract a variety of elites to a coalition.

Alliances of this type were visible in Ceylon and Sierra Leone, to offer but two examples. In Ceylon, the first ruling party, the United Nationalist Party, was organized through a coalition of social notables representing such disparate organizations as the Ceylon National Congress, the Sinhala Maha Sabha (a Sinhalese communal group), the All-Ceylon Muslim League, the Moors' Association, and several Tamil community leaders.[10] The party constitution permitted the coalescing groups to maintain their separate organizations, and they persisted as distinct blocs of interest.[11] This coalition was solidified by a common concern for dominating the government. The party used government positions "to attract support and to forge unity among its leaders and the various social and cultural strata whose interests it articulated."[12] The working committee of the party was made up of the leaders of the associations that founded the party. In a similar way, the Sierra Leone People's Party was a fusion of two associations of Protectorate political elites (one

THE SEARCH FOR POLITICAL STABILITY

founded by chiefs; the other by professional elites) which enabled the Protectorate peoples to break the hold of the Creoles over Sierra Leone politics.[13] Such elite coalitions are not manifested only within the hierarchy of a single party. In Somalia, government dominance was secured by a coalition of three political parties, each representing a different clan group. In Thailand, governments were organized by explicit factions of political elites.

Perhaps a more pervasive basis of coalition is what appears to be a kind of patrimonialism in which elites are integrated in a network around a patrimonial leader, linked to him by their belief in both his personal qualities and in the material rewards to be derived from their association with him.[14] The rewards are the result of the patrimonial leader's selection of his personal followers for patronage positions. As Max Weber has pointed out:

> The object of obedience is the personal authority of the individual which he enjoys by virtue of his traditional status. The organized group exercising authority is, in the simplest case, primarily based on relations of personal loyalty, cultivated through a common process of education. The person exercising authority is not a "superior," but a personal "chief." His administrative staff does not consist primarily of officials, but of personal retainers. Those subject to authority are not "members" of an association, but are either his traditional "comrades" or his "subjects." What determines the relations of the administrative staff to the chief is not the impersonal obligations of office, but personal loyalty to the chief.[15]

Patrimonial elite cohesion is very visible in Morocco, where the political system is fragmented into a variety of primordial and interest factions, each with its own distinctive elite. The king, Hassan II, has sought to control the political system through a wide range of alliances with various elites, based on his power of appointment to virtually every senior governmental position.[16] The palace has become the ultimate source of spoils and patronage, and access to that patronage is necessary if an elite is to satisfy his faction and maintain his leadership status.[17] Elite cohesion is achieved through a multiplicity of linkages between particular elites and the patrimonial leader.

Patrimonial elite integration, however, is not a phenomenon restricted to what appear to be traditional political systems. The emphasis often placed on charismatic leadership in the new states may, in fact, be singling out patrimonial leaders instead.[18] The concern of leaders such as Nkrumah, Senghor, Touré, Bourguiba, and Houphouet-Boigny to stabilize their rule through networks of personal supporters (patrimonial retainers) placed in strategic governmental and political offices is visible in most of the studies of the new state.[19]

Patrimonial relationships can occur within very different institutional settings—within a single institutional hierarchy (such as that of the PDCI in the Ivory Coast or the CPP in Ghana); between institutions (linking a party leader with the leaders of voluntary associations, for example); within traditional or neotraditional palace bureaucratic structures (Burundi until 1967, Ethiopia, Morocco, and Nepal); or within what appear to be modern bureaucratic structures (Pakistan before 1958 and Thailand). In Thailand, dominant coalitions were really congeries of patrimonial factions which were, in turn, integrated by a common aspiration to power. According to Edgar Shore:

> The personal cliques, based on a feudal-like system of personal obligation, provide the principal focus of bureaucratic loyalty and identification. Bonds of reciprocal obligation, reminiscent of earlier patron-client structures in the traditional social system, informally align a number of dependent subordinates with individual political and administrative leaders in more or less cohesive informal structures.[20]

In Pakistan, patrimonial factions constructed by bureaucrat-politicians ultimately fragmented the nationalist party, the Muslim League, in 1956.[21]

Patrimonialism and a common concern for the perquisites

of government do not exhaust the possible sources of elite cohesion. Ideology can link particular elites, as can common party identity or, in fact, coercion. Ghana in the later period of Nkrumah's rule was increasingly an example of the latter. Unable to integrate and organize central political elites through other means, Nkrumah forcibly sought to eliminate from the political system those elites he either could or would not coopt. Such repression secured the compliance of a substantial number of remaining elites.

Cohesion of the political elites, even where it comprises what is in effect a "ruling class," is far more tenuous than is frequently conceptualized. Such cohesion, where it exists, is frequently based on personal loyalties—between the leader at the top and his immediate followers and between central elites. Elite integration is achieved through a series of reciprocity relationships between the various elites.[22] In return for providing support for the center, particular elites derive status and tangible benefits (in the form of political office) and the means (patronage and spoils) to maintain their own followings.

The complexity of these highly personalized alliance patterns within the political center tends to increase in those political systems, such as the one-party states of West Africa, where the ruling political elites are ideologically committed to expanding their control over the society by increasing the scope of government.[23] In effect, such elites seek control by transforming major voluntary associations, such as trade unions, cooperatives, and women's associations, into party wings. Leadership positions in these associations become, in other words, strategic roles within the political center. More often than not, such a transformation is accompanied by the patrimonial leader's attempt to place one of his personal followers in each of these positions. In the Ivory Coast, for example, conflicts after 1959 between the Secretary-General of the PDCI, a leader of the newly created party youth wing, and Houphouet-Boigny culminated in the deposal of the Secretary-General and his replacement by a Houphouet-Boigny loyalist.

The political elites' attempts to organize some basis for coalition among themselves in order to secure dominance of the political center define the boundaries of a political process which is confined to that center. Political leaders seek to consolidate their control over the central government by linking the various groups and institutions within the political center through networks of personal and patronage ties. At the same time, individual elites, utilizing patronage derivative from their positions, seek to maximize their own personal power and followings. The process is reminiscent of the patrimonial systems of medieval Europe which were characterized by

> the struggle between the centralizing efforts of kings, expressed in their attempts to build up bodies of patrimonial retainers responsible to themselves alone, and the decentralizing tendency of subordinate authorities to become locally rooted hereditary lords.[24]

Centralizing tendencies within the political center are constantly countered by the tendency of various elites to become modern equivalents of local hereditary lords. As Reinhard Bendix has noted:

> with the extension and decentralization of a patrimonial regime, the duties of the personal dependents may become attenuated as their actual independence from the master's control increases . . . . it is clear that the extension of patrimonial rule tends to remove the dependent and the political subject from the direct control of the ruler.[25]

This view of the patrimonial regime can be compared to the situation in Algeria during the Ben Bella period:

> Contingent interest groups usually radiate from individuals who either are well-placed in the government or bureaucracy or aspire to be . . . . ministries are apt to form their own interest groups to fulfill their policies and lobby for them with other ministries . . . . The Association of War Veterans, for example, is an extension of the Ministry of

Veterans and Social Affairs . . . . Each [association] is more nearly a network of administrative clients than an institutional or associational interest group.[26]

The political process makes coalitions within the elite tentative, as we noted earlier, and highly vulnerable to fragmentation, as will be explored in the next chapter. The stability of the political center rests upon the elites' perception that the coalitions in which they are participating are yielding benefits for both themselves and their clienteles. The elusiveness of patrimonial authority and the relative scarcity of patronage and spoils to distribute make such perceptions and, therefore, stability problematic at best.

Organizing the Political Periphery

The ability of a regime to survive—let alone to implement various modernization programs—depends upon its ability to expand its authority beyond the center and to consolidate its control over the periphery. Such consolidation is, to a considerable degree, assisted by the dependency of local elites on centrally controlled resources. The central elites, in varying degrees, determine the flow of such resources to the periphery through their enforcement of central regulations and their control over government revenue and patronage. This ability to control resources, even where it is limited, not only structures center-periphery relationships but also—because one set of local elites can be favored over another—tends to shape local power relations as well.

Local elites and groups are not without bargaining power, however. They can utilize their own personal financial resources and their traditional ties of kinship and clientele within the local political system either to facilitate or to hamper political consolidation. Moreover, while local elites are often dependent upon centrally controlled resources in order to sustain their status, the effective use of those resources to achieve consolidation is

57

no less dependent upon the willingness and the capabilities of the local elites.

Organizing the periphery, then, involves a subtle interplay of central and local political processes. The strategic calculations of central and local elites, for example, may conflict. Conflicts within the center or within the local political system may alter the interdependency. Conflicts within the center may make the central elites disinclined to take account of local needs; conflicts within the periphery may produce power relationships that are not recognized by center elites.

The relationship between the central political system and the local subsystems has traditionally been difficult for the social scientist to conceptualize. In the first place, there is what Martin Kilson has called the "boundary problem": the inability of "political actors . . . to distinguish functionally the secular and sacred criteria of political choice and action."[27] Central elites are often reluctant to accommodate local elites' demands because they perceive such demands as being both primordial and parochial and, hence, antinational, and they fear any accommodation will be viewed as a concession to antinationalism.[28] The boundary problem, however, is not confined to the political actors themselves. Social scientists, especially political scientists, are often equally prone to identifying primordialism and parochialism as deterrents to nation-building. Such forces are seen to represent continuing subnational identification which stands in the way of a truly national political system.[29] As a result, economic and political conflicts between center and periphery—which may or may not have a primordial component—are often viewed only in terms of nationalism versus primordialism, nationalists versus parochials.

The term "periphery," as it is being used here, represents an effort to establish a dimension of analysis distinct from the question of nationalism versus subnationalism.[30] Regardless of how strong a "national" political system is, a political periphery—removed from the central institutions of authority—persists, shaped by local social and political institutions and local conflicts.

THE SEARCH FOR POLITICAL STABILITY

Recently, there have been efforts to conceptualize center-periphery relationships in terms of one or more crises that appear to have arisen historically in the process of political development.[31] The descriptions of such crises—particularly of those concerning identity, legitimacy, participation, and penetration—depict, in a variety of ways, the gap between center and periphery and the difficulties in overcoming that gap. The crisis scheme is a suggestive framework for the study of political development, although the sequence of the crises and the relationships between them remain vague, as their formulators admit.[32] Yet, the crisis scheme tends to reify the gap between center and periphery and to gloss over the variety of linkages that may already exist between the two. The crucial problem faced by the political elites may be, not so much to "penetrate" modern institutions into an inert social mass and then to mobilize that social mass, as to recognize the existence of a highly syncretic society (or set of societies) interlinked in a variety of ways and to give that complex set of linkages some coherence.

Sources of Center-Periphery Cohesion

The transition from nationalist movement to independent government is invariably accompanied by the central elites' efforts to expand their influence and to control the periphery. After independence, the segmentary character of the "nationalist movement" almost immediately undermines its unity (if such a thing really ever existed), and different means of integrating the various segments must be sought.

In studying this transition, scholars have chosen to emphasize ideology and charisma. Both, in effect, represent extraordinary means of regenerating the unity identified with the nationalist movement. Implicit in the emphasis on ideology and charisma is the argument that the cultural and social chasm between elites and nonelites is so enormous that it can be bridged only by singularly extraordinary means. Yet, as the analysis of nationalist movements suggests, ties do exist between elites and nonelites. Thus, nationalist elites—such as Paul Bomani in Tanzania, to return to an earlier example—assume senior governmental and political positions and serve as linkages between their particular followings and the center, acting as patron on their followers' behalf in their dealings with party and bureaucracy, communicating new political goals and norms, and, at times, intervening in the local political process. In Ceylon, the elites who ran as United National Party candidates in the first general election, and who emerged as the party and government center, were linked to clusters of locally influential contacts.[33]

Such personal linkages appear to be pervasive in the underdeveloped states. Although most recent research has tended to focus on patron-client bonds as the most common type of linkage, other dyadic relationships have been suggested—alliances between two individuals of equal status, patron-client relationships in which the exchanges and obligations are very limited, particular kinship and ethnic linkages, and so forth.[34] When financial resources and patronage are available to central elites, they can use these linkages, first, to distribute goods and services to the periphery and, second, to secure a stable personal following (clientele). A reciprocity relationship emerges. In return for patronage and other favors, a clientele provides status for the elite and, when necessary, electoral support.[35]

The reciprocity characteristic of these linkages has led to a depiction of the political parties in underdeveloped states as organizations resembling the political machines so widely discussed in the literature on American political parties.[36] Such party machines are built around reciprocity relationships and function, not to frame policies or discipline members, but rather to win elections and, as a result, jobs for their members. Thus, in India,

> Congress party leaders, in order to succeed politically, are concerned, first and foremost, with doing whatever is necessary to adapt the party to its environment . . . . The Congress is primarily concerned with recruiting members

and winning support. It does not mobilize; it aggregates. It does not seek to innovate; it seeks to adapt. Though a few Congressmen dream of transforming the countryside, in practice most Congressmen are concerned simply with winning elections. . . . While India's national government and the bureaucracy tend to be developmentally oriented, local politicians are very much concerned with questions of distribution. The ideology of Congress, which conceives of socialism as social and especially as economic equity, makes distribution politics legitimate. While it is customary to distinguish between parties of patronage and parties of ideology, what is striking here is the extent which ideology—in this instance, the appeal to equity—is used to support patronage.[37]

As another example, in northern Nigeria,

The structure of the NPC (Northern People's Congress) fits conveniently into this structure of traditional relationships in at least two important respects. First, by virtue of the powers it exercised through the control of the government, the party was a principal agency of patronage offices, loans, scholarships, contracts, and other opportunities sought by the upwardly mobile. This could be accomplished either directly and formally or indirectly through the medium of the party or ex-party men who dominated the public boards, corporations, or commissions. Second, (and of greater consequence in terms of winning mass support), the interlocking directorate of local administrative and party personnel inescapably bound humble persons to traditionally august figures in their capacity as party men. The dependency that derived from the vast network of clientage relationships inherent in the traditional society was transferred to the party. . . .[38]

Elsewhere, too, parties are seen as congeries of national, regional, and local elites linked by a variety of personal relationships. Such relationships act as communication channels for the distribution of patronage and spoils. Patronage structures these machines, gaining support for them because they act as sources of material rewards. The machine is, in effect, often a multitiered pyramid of personal followings.

61

Some effort has been made to distinguish between those party machines built on existing personal linkages and traditional deference patterns between elite and mass (the Northern People's Congress in Nigeria is frequently cited as this type of machine, as is, to a lesser degree, the Sierra Leone People's Party) and the more orthodox machines in which vertical alliances are maintained through material inducements alone (the PDCI of the Ivory Coast is offered as a typical example of this type).[39] In reality, however, it seems difficult to maintain the distinction. Orthodox machines, at times, seem to encompass linkages that are far more than materially based—ethnic group support for a particular leader, for example—and, in fact, it appears that a party can be built on both types of linkage. In Burma, during the 1950's, the Anti-Fascist People's Freedom League (always called the AFPFL) appeared to be based on existing patron-client links in the countryside and on more limited, materially based solidarities in the towns.[40]

The machine concept can be elaborated on somewhat. In the first place, political machines need not be confined to political parties.[41] In Morocco, the king's personal power of appointment goes beyond the senior governmental offices to include "a sprawling system of contractual arrangements . . . by which large numbers of middle-range and even petty bureaucrats are able to adjust their pay and promotion scales outside the normal Civil Service procedure."[42] As a result, the king has a personal machine. By manipulating resources in the favor of particular elites, Hassan has attracted their support and through them gained access to and control of the periphery.

At times, party machines mask or coexist with personal machines. Patrimonial relationships may underlie the efforts to organize a political party. Central elites may use appointments to consolidate their own personal control of the party and of the party machine. In the Ivory Coast, personal representatives of Houphouet-Boigny selected men whom they knew and trusted as the secretaries-general of the intermediary party branches, the *sous-sections*.[43] These men, in turn, selected individuals for other party offices at that level.[44] What ultimately emerged was a personal network linked to Houphouet-Boigny, as well as a party organization.

Machines can be organized by bureaucratic elites as well, developing outward and downward along personal linkages between bureaucrat-patrons, clients at lower levels in the bureaucracy, and the general population of government. In Thailand, senior bureaucrats often act as patrons for particular middle-level bureaucrats, who do the same for particular lower-level bureaucrats. Each, in turn, is linked to local clienteles who request patronage.

Second, the machine concept really exaggerates the coherence of the various personal linkages between center and periphery. Even where relatively well-organized party machines exist, such as the Congress Party of India or the PDCI, local elites and their followings do not remain in position in the party hierarchy. Instead, depending on the resource needed, they may establish other linkages—to other political elites, removed from the ordinary party hierarchy or even outside the party; to bureaucratic elites; to economic elites. Machines—personal, party, and bureaucratic—coexist and intertwine with one another. Commenting on party politics in the Philippines, Carl Landé has written:

> political leaders wander into and out of parties with their personal followers in tow, feeling no strong obligation, and being under no real pressure, to support their party mates. Party membership is not a category but a matter of degree.
>
> If one wishes to discover the real framework upon which election campaigns are built, one must turn away from political parties and focus one's attention upon individual candidates and vertical chains of leadership and followership into which they arrange themselves at any given point in time. While tending to tie together persons who claim the same party label, these chains must in fact be viewed as independent structures resembling a network of strong vines which variously cling to or twist back and forth between two great but hollow trees [the political parties].[45]

If we augment this analogy by adding additional "vines" representing the sometimes momentary clienteles of bureaucratic elites and by noting that the various vines intersect and grow into one another, the complexity of center-periphery linkages and of the machines begins to emerge.

This already considerable degree of complexity increases when a regime seeks to expand its control of the periphery through the deconcentration of the central party and the central government from the center of the periphery—i.e., the posting of centrally appointed party and bureaucratic cadres in political and administrative positions in the hinterland.[46] In theory, deconcentration, which includes augmenting the powers of central appointees while weakening the powers of local party branches and governments, expands the number of services for which local populations must look to a representative of the center and permits, as a result, "a substantial increase in the center's potential for control over the localities."[47]

Deconcentration has become characteristic of the political process in the new states.[48] In the mobilization party-states, in particular, the central elites have made an almost continuous effort to establish a hierarchy of appointed officials who would be beholden to the party national office and who would not have to rely on the good will of district and local organizations.[49] In Ghana, the CPP's consolidation of a one-party state was accompanied by a move to place the local CPP branches under firmer control. The local party organization was dissolved and replaced by district and regional party branches run by appointed district and regional commissioners.[50]

At times, the center, in the guise of an administrative or technical field agent, seems pervasive. Commenting on the "myriad ways" that the Burmese village of Nondwin was affected by government and administration, Manning Nash has noted:

> The ties between villages and other levels of government are many and diverse. The most obvious connections are through taxes and police and court agencies. Tax officials, policemen, and soldiers come to the village in the normal course of business and deal with the villagers either individually or through the thugyi [headman] and council

of elders . . . . The departments of roads, forests, and agriculture provide the services appropriate to their domain . . . . The villagers must get permission to cut certain size trees and, sometimes, get seed money or money loans from an agency of the agricultural department . . . . The government also provides some minimal medical services which the people frequently use . . . . The education of the youth of the village is now largely in the hands of the state agency.[51]

Because it increases the number of individuals who have access to some resources, deconcentration tends to expand the number of clientele structures linking center and periphery. Local administrative agents, by virtue of their contacts with the central government, tend to become quasi-patrons in their own right. Perhaps more important, party elites removed from existing clientele relationships often emerge as patrons and brokers. Myron Weiner, discussing the Congress Party's reaction to the expansion of government machinery for economic and social development, noted:

> The party has responded to this expansion of administrative activities by creating a class of "expeditors" who serve as a link between administrators and citizens. To say "create," however, implies a conscious decision and a program of action which is quite misleading. It is also misleading to assume that the role is a new one. To the contrary, there was a class of individuals under British rule who had access to local administration and used that access to further their own or their group's interests. But prior to 1937 (when the Congress gained control over several state governments and actually exercised political control at the state level) relatively few people within the Congress performed this function. When the party took power those who performed expediting roles joined the party. . . .[52]

In summary, the linkages between center and periphery encompass a variety of personal relationships. Such linkages are organized in terms of the central elites' control over the allocation of government resources and services. In theory, at least, their allocation of resources and services to the periphery is directed in such a way as to maximize support for the regime. In practice, such support is, more often than not, highly tenuous.

Sources of Center-Periphery Conflict

If the linkages between center and periphery are frequently understated, the nature of conflict between center and periphery is equally misunderstood, although in a different way. As noted earlier, social scientists often identify parochialism simply in primordial or, to use a more common word, traditional terms. Conflict between center and periphery, in other words, is frequently reduced to nationalism versus subnationalism (tribalism, castism, and the like) or, more globally, modernity versus tradition. Hence, the problem of organizing the periphery becomes primarily one of reducing the autonomy of traditional authorities, political movements, and groups within the geographical boundaries of the new state. Although the dichotomy between tradition and modernity tends to be overstressed in such analyses,[53] the importance of such conflicts cannot be denied. The competition between the CPP and the various ethnic political parties in Ghana (especially the Northern People's Party and the National Liberation Movement) is but one example of such conflict.[54] Yet, the problem of center-periphery linkage goes beyond this relatively simple version of the integration crisis. Even when such linkages are present and the authority of the center is accepted, the center may not be able to consolidate its control over the periphery. Conflicts between center and periphery may be not so much a question of nationalism versus some form of separatism as a question of managing a highly segmented political system.

The complexity of the linkages between center and periphery—a complexity often exacerbated by the central elites' efforts to expand their control over the periphery—is a principal cause of this managerial problem. Few regimes have been able to define adequately a hierarchy among the various technical,

THE SEARCH FOR POLITICAL STABILITY

bureaucratic, and political elites who are intertwined in the various connections between center and periphery. Deconcentration is seldom accompanied by explicit decisions as to who outranks whom. Conflicts over such ranking and over the authority and patronage such ranking brings—between appointed officials, between appointed officials and elected officials, between local political elites and local bureaucratic and technical elites, and so forth—become endemic to the political process.

This is not simply a problem of the centralizing elites' failing to establish a status hierarchy in the periphery. Few regimes actually possess the resources to dictate such a hierarchy. Since the economic pie is small and growing only slowly, it is difficult to distribute patronage as a means of centralizing authority.[55] This incapacity is characteristic not only of the political elites but of bureaucratic elites as well. Commenting on local bureaucrats in the Ivory Coast, one scholar has noted that the "proliferation [of subprefectures, the local official government posts] in recent years has unavoidably entailed the posting of minimally required personnel with scant resources. Outside the major towns, a subprefecture often consists of little more than a single clerk frequently lacking even a typewriter. . . ."[56] The political machines—whether personal, party, or bureaucratic—are all vulnerable to what Bienen has called the "vicious circle of underdevelopment—limited resources—weak organization—limited resources."[57]

The lines of authority and hierarchy in the periphery are blurred. Appointed officials, in theory representatives of the center, are, in actuality, very much dependent upon the local constituency's cooperation if they are to achieve any assigned goals at all. As a result, officials tend to develop their own local followings (patrimonies), misusing what government resources there are, misdirecting revenues into their own pockets, and misapplying regulations in order to build their own machines.[58] When this happens, linkages between center and periphery can almost disappear.

The blurred authority and the complex linkage patterns have another consequence which, in turn, only exacerbates these problems. Because authority is so diffused at the local level, individuals seeking access to the center often try to bypass existing personal, bureaucratic, and political machines in order to deal with the central elites on a personal basis. Existing machines, in other words, are short-circuited; the available patronage and spoils are frequently delivered through momentary personal connections rather than along established lines. The complexity of the center-periphery linkages is continuously increased by the efforts of those seeking favors to find new patrons. Thus, in Ghana,

> Elaborate machinery was established to coordinate the activities of the [various local] groups, but there was a great tendency to bypass this machinery and to appeal to headquarters, the regional commissioner, or to Nkrumah himself. Persons claiming to be "holier" than others in the sense that they had access to Nkrumah constantly ignored the usual channels and the *Party Chronicle* warned repeatedly that "only the most serious, intricate and stubborn issues affecting major policy are to be referred to the National Secretariat. Every trivial matter referred . . . to Accra is an indication that someone is not doing his duty or that a party member is violating party procedure."[59]

Not all sources of center-periphery divergence lie in the periphery. Central elites, for example, may pursue inconsistent policies or change policies in a relatively short period of time. In Senegal, after a period of party-building, the Senghor regime implemented a series of reforms that, in effect, sought to strengthen the presence of the bureaucracy in the periphery while diminishing that of the dominant party, the *Union Progressiste Sénégalaise*.[60] The bureaucracy received additional authority vis-à-vis local party elites, and local party elites were deprived of patronage powers. The result was a weakening of the UPS party branches in the name of organizing the government along lines most conducive to supporting Senegal's development goals.[61]

Conflicts among the central elites may undermine the various links between center and periphery as well. Discussing these links in Ghana, Martin Kilson has noted that competition and tension between upper-status, university elites—needed to run the government—and second-echelon CPP functionaries ultimately led to the central leadership's transformation of voluntary associations (trade unions and the like) into party wings, thereby giving the CPP functionaries national party posts.[62] While the transformation succeeded in achieving this goal (at the expense of considerable factionalism), it was ultimately harmful in terms of center-periphery relationships. In the first place, the transformation of voluntary associations into paragovernmental organizations tended to undercut their effectiveness because they became far less cognizant of their members' interests.[63] Second, such a transformation introduced, into an already confused setting, a new set of institutional and personal linkages. The United Ghana Farmers Council Cooperatives, for example, eventually employed over 3,000 politically relevant functionaries, such as regional officers, district officers, marketing officers, depot officers, and secretary receivers.[64]

In India, to take another example, conflicts within the Congress High Command after 1966 appear to have severely limited the ability of the central elites to influence state politics. Prior to this period, the High Command seems to have succeeded in preventing the constant factionalism at the lower levels from fragmenting the party (forcing accommodations between factions, etc.); but after 1967 especially, the High Command was incapacitated by its own disputes and was thus less effective in forcing unity compromises in the state and district parties. The result was a rapid escalation of personal machines (factions) breaking away from the Congress. The periphery became more chaotic than ever.

In the final analysis, the relationship between center and periphery in the underdeveloped state is almost paradoxical. On one hand, a multitude of linkages exist between center and periphery. The complex networks linking the two are constantly changing and being added to. At the same time, even the more organized machines, such as the Tanganyikan African National Union, are "congeries of regional, district, and subdistrict

69

organizations which communicate with each other and with Dar es Salaam only intermittently."[65] The networks are highly personal, dependent on patronage and subtle power relationships in the center and the periphery.

The habit of discussing politics in terms of discrete actors —governmental institutions, political parties, interest groups —dies hard. And yet, that habit, more often than not, causes one to overlook a key distinction of politics in the underdeveloped states—their amorphousness. What appear to be institutions are, at their cores, often little more than coalitions of elites and, at their outer reaches, complex sets of highly personal face-to-face relationships, all momentarily integrated by access to government and its patronage. Institution-building seldom results in a durable set of political procedures and behavior in the sense that Samuel Huntington has characterized the process: "Institutions are stable, valued, recurring patterns of behavior."[66] Institutions are more likely to be facades for transient and often intermittent patterns of interaction among central elites and between them and the periphery. The personalism that permeates underdeveloped political systems seems, at times, to yield a political process that is not simply uninstitutionalized but, in fact, hostile to institutionalization.

NOTES

1. These concepts are suggested by Edward Shils, who defines a center as "the centre of the order of symbols, of values and beliefs, which govern the society. . . . It is the structure of activities, of roles and persons, within the network of institutions. . . . The power of the ruling class derives from its incumbency of certain key positions in the central institutional system." Edward Shils, "Centre and Periphery," *The Logic of Personal Knowledge: Essays Presented to Michael Polanyi* (London: Routledge and Kegan Paul, 1961), pp. 117, 125.

2. Aristide Zolberg, *One-Party Government in the Ivory Coast* (Princeton: Princeton University Press, 1964), pp. 323-324.

3. See, for example, David Apter, *The Politics of Modernization*

THE SEARCH FOR POLITICAL STABILITY

(Chicago: University of Chicago Press, 1967), especially pp. 313-356.

4. David Apter, *Ghana in Transition* (New York: Atheneum, 1963).

5. Henry Bienen, *Tanzania: Party Transformation and Economic Development* (Princeton: Princeton University Press, 1970), p. 5.

6. Aristide Zolberg, *Creating Political Order: The Party-States of West Africa* (Chicago: Rand-McNally and Co., 1966), p. 138.

7. For such studies, see, especially, Zolberg, *Creating Political Order* and Bienen, *Tanzania*.

8. Rajni Kothari, *Politics in India* (Boston: Little, Brown and Company, 1970), p. 159.

9. Because of their recentness and increasing importance and because of the very different perception that most military elites have about this process of coalition, military regimes will be examined separately, although some relevant comparisons are discussed in this chapter. See Chapter 5.

10. On the Ceylonese party system, see Calvin Woodward, *The Growth of a Party System in Ceylon* (Providence: Brown University Press, 1969).

11. United Nationalist Party, *Manifesto and Constitution* (1947), articles 3 and 9.

12. Woodward, p. 73.

13. On Sierra Leone, see Martin Kilson, *Political Change in a West African State* (Cambridge, Mass.: Harvard University Press, 1966); and John R. Cartwright, *Politics in Sierra Leone 1947-1967* (Toronto: University of Toronto Press, 1970).

14. Patrimonial authority is explored by Max Weber in *The Theory of Social and Economic Organization*, trans. by Talcott Parsons (New York: Free Press, 1957). Weber defines patrimonialism as existing "where authority is primarily oriented to tradition but in its exercise makes a claim to full personal powers" (p. 347).

15. *Ibid.*, p. 341.

16. John Waterbury, *Commander of the Faithful* (New York: Columbia University Press, 1970), p. 270.

17. *Ibid.*

18. Patrimonialism as a theoretical concept to better explain linkages within what were originally perceived to be highly monolithic parties was initially suggested by Zolberg, *Creating Political Order*, pp. 141-142, and especially by Guenther Roth, "Personal Rulership, Patrimonialism, and Empire-Building in the New States," *World Politics*, XX, 2 (1968), 194-203. Zolberg seems to limit patrimonialism to situations where charisma has become "routinized." J. C. Willame, *Patrimonialism and Political Change in the Congo* (Stanford: Stanford University Press, 1972), also attempts to utilize this concept. Willame, however, restricts the "patrimonial era" in the Congo to the period when private armies were clashing with one another (1960-1965).

19. See the previously cited studies of these leaders and their

states. H. L. Bretton, *The Rise and Fall of Kwame Nkrumah* (London: Praeger, 1967), despite its exaggeration of Nkrumah's personal rulership, is also informative.

20. Edgar Shore, "The Thai Bureaucracy," *Administrative Science Quarterly*, V (June 1960), 70. For a detailed study of Thailand, see David A. Wilson, *Politics in Thailand* (Ithaca: Cornell University Press, 1962).

21. This argument is developed in Gerald A. Heeger, "Bureaucracy, Political Parties, and Political Development," *World Politics*, XXV, 4 (July 1973), 600-607.

22. The reciprocity principle was first suggested by Kilson, *Political Change in a West African State* (Cambridge, Mass.: Harvard University Press, 1966). See especially pp. 252-280.

23. The one-party ideology has elicited much comment. See, in particular, Charles Andrain, "Democracy and Socialism: Ideologies of African Leaders," in David E. Apter, ed., *Ideology and Discontent* (New York: Free Press, 1964), pp. 157-169; Zolberg, *Creating Political Order*, pp. 37-65; James Heaphey, "The Organization of Egypt: Inadequacies of a Nonpolitical Model for Nation-Building," *World Politics*, XVIII, 2 (1966), 177-183. See also Bernard Crick, *In Defence of Politics* (Chicago: University of Chicago Press, 1972).

24. Lloyd Fallers and Audrey Richards, eds., *The King's Men* (London: Oxford University Press, 1964), p. 99.

25. Reinhard Bendix, *Max Weber: An Intellectual Portrait* (Garden City, N.Y.: Doubleday and Co., 1962), p. 336.

26. Clement H. Moore, *Politics in North Africa* (Boston: Little, Brown and Company, 1970), p. 204.

27. Martin Kilson, "The Grassroots in Ghanaian Politics," in Philip Foster and Aristide R. Zolberg, eds., *Ghana and the Ivory Coast* (Chicago: University of Chicago Press, 1971), p. 116.

28. For a reflection on the policies that often flow from this boundary problem, see McKim Marriott, "Cultural Policies in the New States," in Clifford Geertz, ed., *Old Societies and New States* (New York: Free Press, 1963).

29. See especially Clifford Geertz, "The Integrative Revolution: Primordial Sentiments and Civic Politics in the New States," in *ibid.*, pp. 105-157.

30. Indeed, *when* the periphery (or part of it) becomes subnational and *under what conditions* are critical questions lost when the two terms are equated with one another. This and related issues are discussed in Chapter 4.

31. The crisis framework is explored in Leonard Binder, et al., *Crises and Sequences in Political Development* (Princeton: Princeton University Press, 1971). See also Raymond Grew, "Crises of Political Development," paper delivered at the 1972 annual meeting of the American Political Science Association, Washington, D.C.

32. Sidney Verba, "Sequences and Development," in Binder, et al., pp. 283-316.

33. Woodward, p. 178.

34. See, for example, Carl H. Landé, "Networks and Groups in Southeast Asia: Some Observations in the Group Theory of Politics," *American Political Science Review* LXVII, 1 (1973), 103-127.

35. Lemarchand, in this regard, noted: "Political competence meant in essence the ability to keep in tow a reliable clientele through the dispensation of prebends." René Lemarchand, "Political Clientelism and Ethnicity in Tropical Africa: Competing Solidarities in Nation-Building," *American Political Science Review*, LXVI, 1 (1972), 79.

36. On the American political machine, see C. E. Merriam and H. F. Gosnell, *The American Party System* (New York: Macmillan and Co., 1949); and Edward Banfield, *Political Influence* (New York: Free Press, 1961). Henry Bienen has been the most prolific proponent of the machine model's applicability to African political parties. See his *Tanzania*, pp. 3-15; his "Political Machines in Africa," in Michael Lofchie, ed., *The State of Nations: Constraints on Development in Independent Africa* (Berkeley and Los Angeles: University of California Press, 1971); and his "One-Party Systems in Africa," in Samuel P. Huntington and Clement H. Moore, eds., *Authoritarian Politics in Modern Society* (New York: Basic Books, 1970), pp. 99-127.

37. Myron Weiner, *Party-Building in a New Nation* (Chicago: University of Chicago Press, 1967), pp. 14-15, 473.

38. C. S. Whitaker, *The Politics of Tradition* (Princeton: Princeton University Press, 1970), p. 375.

39. Lemarchand, p. 86.

40. For material on the AFPFL and Burma, see Frank N. Trager, *Burma: From Kingdom to Republic* (New York: Frederick A. Praeger, 1966), pp. 166-214; and Richard Butwell, *U Nu of Burma* (Stanford: Stanford University Press, 1966), pp. 146-171.

41. The equation of the two appears to have its origins in the fact that American machines were almost always political parties. Thus, Banfield defined machines as "*parties* [italics mine] which rely characteristically upon the attraction of material rewards rather than enthusiasm for political principles" (p. 237).

42. Waterbury, p. 269. Similar palace machines were visible in Ethiopia, Iran, and Burundi between 1962 and 1968.

43. Richard E. Stryker, "Political and Administrative Linkage in the Ivory Coast," in Foster and Zolberg, pp. 86-87.

44. *Ibid.*, p. 87.

45. Landé, p. 116.

46. "Deconcentration" is traditionally applied only to administrative and technical cadres. See, for example, M. J. Campbell, et al., *The Structure of Local Government in West Africa* (The Hague: M. Nijhoff, 1965). Because we are arguing that the use of party appointees at the local level is also frequently an effort to augment the power of the center party at the expense of the local branches, the term seems equally applicable to the political party as well.

47. Zolberg, *Creating Political Order*, p. 115.

48. For an excellent comparative study of such efforts in three states, see Douglas Ashford, *National Development and Local Reform* (Princeton: Princeton University Press, 1967).

49. See, for example, Bienen, *Tanzania*, especially pp. 112-157.

50. Dennis L. Cohen, "The Convention People's Party of Ghana: Representational or Solidarity Party," *Canadian Journal of African Studies*, IV, 2 (1970), 177.

51. Manning Nash, *The Golden Road to Modernity* (New York: John Wiley and Sons, 1965), pp. 93-94. Of course, not all villages in all states see such activity, but it is worth noting that Nash is writing of a period when politics in the political center was in chaos and on the verge of a military coup.

52. Myron Weiner, "Role Performance and the Development of Modern Political Parties: The Indian Case," *Journal of Politics*, XXVI, 4 (November 1964), 835.

53. These concepts are scrutinized in Lloyd I. Rudolph and Susanne Hoeber Rudolph, *The Modernity of Tradition* (Chicago: University of Chicago Press, 1967).

54. See Dennis Austin, *Politics in Ghana, 1946-1960* (London: Oxford University Press, 1970), pp. 250-315, for a discussion of these conflicts.

55. Bienen, "Political Machines in Africa," p. 204.

56. Stryker, p. 93.

57. Bienen, *Tanzania*, p. 412.

58. The role corruption plays in these societies is a complex subject. For a reflection on the topic, see James C. Scott, "The Analysis of Corruption in Developing Nations," *Comparative Studies in Society and History*, XI, 3 (June 1969), 315-341; and his *Comparative Political Corruption* (Englewood Cliffs, N.J.: Prentice-Hall, 1972).

59. Selwyn Ryan, "The Theory and Practice of African One Partyism: The CPP Re-examined," *Canadian Journal of African Studies*, IV, 2 (1970), 157; quoting *Party Chronicle*, XXXVII (June 1964).

60. Clement Cottingham, "Political Consolidation and Centre-Local Relations in Senegal," *Canadian Journal of African Studies*, IV, 1 (1970), 103.

61. *Ibid*.

62. Kilson, "The Grassroots in Ghanaian Politics," p. 119.

63. For one study of a functional group's relationships with a "party-state," see William Tordoff, "Trade Unionism in Tanzania," *Journal of Development Studies*, II, 4 (1966), 408-430.

64. Kilson, p. 120.

65. Bienen, *Tanzania*, p. 413.

66. Samuel Huntington, *Political Order in Changing Societies* (New Haven: Yale University Press, 1968), p. 12.

4

The Politics of Instability

In recent years, almost every underdeveloped state has experienced political instability in one form or another—military coups and mutinies, insurrections, political assassinations, rioting, chaotic factional conflict among leaders, and so forth. Such instability has occurred, so it has been lamented, with "little regard for the social scientists" in that "the incidence of conflict and disorder appears unrelated to such variables as type of colonial experience, size, number of parties, absolute level or rate of economic and social development."[1]

What are the sources of instability? The answers provided have possessed a remarkable consistency over the past decade and a half: underdeveloped states are instable because their political institutions lack the capability to deal with the consequences of social and economic changes. This argument can be broken down into several propositions:

1. *The effects of modernization are highly unbalanced in underdeveloped societies*.

Although the new political units provided a territorial mold within which social, economic, political, and cultural changes that accompanied colonialization occurred, we are becoming aware that these processes, although related, did not necessarily vary "rhythmically," i.e., at the same rate. . . .[2]

Perhaps the major characteristic of the process of modernization is that it has been unbalanced . . . especially in the relations of the processes of change and transition between the "central" and the local levels.[3]

2. *Modernization means a rapid escalation of demands especially by those modern groups upon which the new political system is most dependent.*

Social and economic change . . . multiply political demands, broaden political participation. These changes undermine traditional sources of political authority and traditional political institutions; they enormously complicate the problems of creating new bases of political association and new political institutions.[4]

In whatever country it occurs, social mobilization brings with it an expansion of the politically relevant strata of the population . . . . As people are uprooted from their physical and intellectual isolation in their immediate localities, from their old habits and traditions . . . they experience drastic changes in their needs. They may now come to need provisions for housing and employment, for social security . . . medical care . . . succor against the risks of cyclical or seasonal unemployment . . . instruction for themselves and education for their children. They need, in short, a wide range and large amounts of new government services.[5]

[A] major source of challenge involves three crucial categories of individuals: civilian employees of government, men in uniform, and youths . . . . government employees often constitute in terms of income and prestige the most privileged group in society, after the politicians themselves . . . . Because of their very occupation and training, government employees have internalized the style of life of their European predecessors; they feel that on the grounds of native ability and training they are qualified to rule rather than merely to execute policies; rapid promotions only lead to higher aspirations among those who have already been promoted and among those left behind. . . . Men in uniform tend to act very much like other government employees . . . .
    . . . the intergenerational gap can be noticed in almost

every institutional sphere. . . . [Such] conflict is exacerbated by the fact that youthful discontent tends to be manifested not only by individual deviance from established norms, but also in the appearance of age-homogeneous movements and organizations, functional equivalents of the familiar youth gangs of industrialized societies, which tend to maintain a distinctive subculture and to act autonomously in the political sphere.[6]

3. *The escalation of demands and the competition of different communities for scarce resources have politicized communal divisions and exacerbated tensions between communities.*

Pre-existing distinctions between groups in Africa were usually supplemented by others stemming from the uneven impact of European-generated change . . . . In general, almost any difference between two groups can become politically significant . . . .[7]

It is against this backdrop of social mobilization and a highly competitive modern sector that communal conflict in culturally plural societies must be understood . . . . In culturally plural societies, citizens tend to perceive their competitive world through a communal prism and to be responsive to communal appeals. Communalism therefore becomes a matter of opportunism. It matters not that, in any given competition, communal criteria are inappropriate to the determination of the outcome and may not in fact have been operative. What is important is that the personal fortunes of individuals are generally believed to depend on their communal origins and connections.[8]

4. *The modern political institutions are too new to possess the capacity to respond to the escalation of demands.*

The political backwardness of the country in terms of political institutionalization, moreover, makes it difficult if not impossible for the demands upon the government to be expressed through legitimate channels and to be moderated and aggregated within the political system. Hence the sharp increase in political participation gives rise to political instability.[9]

77

Another proposition is often appended to this general argument. Instability is frequently attributed to leaders who have been less than competent "in the sense that they possessed too few modernizing attitudes and formal skills for the function of governing."[10]

The argument laid out here by example is a suggestive one and conjures up the image of a fragile political center being overwhelmed by the traditionalism of the periphery. There are some difficulties, however, both in the argument and in the image.

In the first place, the emphasis on institutionalization or institutional capability contains the bias noted earlier in this study: that change is inevitable and needs only to be managed correctly. Instability is thought to be inevitable in the sense that it is the culmination of confused or corrupt leadership, ill-planned economic ventures, inadequately controlled mass participation, and so forth. At the same time it is not inevitable in the sense that all of these ills can be changed—new leaders selected, better plans made, more discipline imposed. There is, however, little evidence to suggest that this latter statement is true. The empirical evidence of instability is overwhelming. Leaders seem never to be good enough, nor plans incisive enough. The question arises as to what degree political instability in the underdeveloped state is inevitable, regardless of the wisdom of its managers. The political process characteristic of the underdeveloped state is inherently instable. The tenuous cohesion of political elites within the political center, the transient nature of their alliances, and the vulnerability of those alliances to personal conflict between elites seem almost inevitably to undermine any political institutions.

Second, the concept of demand escalation, while theoretically impressive, is somewhat blurred in reality. How much escalation is too much? How do we know? Only after a system has collapsed and left us with insufficient data to offer other explanations? More often than not, it appears that the center is not so much assaulted by the demands and participation

THE POLITICS OF INSTABILITY

engendered by modernization as it is wracked by personalism and factionalism.

The difference between this proposition and the prevailing argument is subtle but important. Rather than arguing that participation *per se* is the source of instability, it suggests that the political elites are themselves the major source of that instability. The tenuousness of their cohesion, coupled with the decentralizing tendencies present in the political system, makes the center inherently instable. The expansion of the number of functions undertaken by the government only exacerbates this problem by increasing the number of power bases in the political center.

Intra-elite conflict in underdeveloped states has a massing effect that has traditionally been associated with segmentary systems. Groups and elites related to the individual elites immediately concerned in a dispute tend to be drawn into that dispute until several large factions emerge.[11] Such conflict engenders a kind of faction-building process as conflicting elites seek to mobilize wider bases of personal support. Competing elites seek to consolidate what are, in effect, their own patrimonies.

Such faction- or patrimony-building can manifest itself in a variety of ways. Political elites may utilize ideological appeals or appeals to primordial ties in an effort to establish and to maintain their followings. They may seek to expand their personal alliances to include bureaucratic and military elites. Intra-elite conflict and factionalism, in other words, are frequently intertwined with such phenomena as communalism and military intervention.

Factionalism and Patrimony-Building

That factionalism among the political elites of the underdeveloped states is endemic is without dispute. There is a tendency, however, to define the factions in such a way that the

79

divisions come to reflect almost inevitable and irreconcilable differences. One example of this is the analysis of intra-elite conflict in purely ideological terms. John Kautsky, for example, discussing post-independence conflict among the nationalist elites (whom he calls "the modernizers"), pointed to ideological divisions first.[12] Other supposedly inevitable cleavages are also emphasized—e.g., generational conflicts within the nationalist movement, conflicts between elites from different ethnic backgrounds.

The problem with such generalizations is not that the divisions among the elites are not real and meaningful—they often are—but that these divisions are not inevitable and foreordained.[13] Modernization tends to multiply the possibilities for social identities—particular as well as national. Social and political identities in the underdeveloped states are numerous, largely inchoate, and, consequently, amorphous. The real question is not whether social cleavages will manifest themselves but, rather, along which lines of cleavage will salient political divisions appear. In order to understand conflict among the political elites, it appears necessary to start not with their social, economic, and ideological differences but with their attempt to make such cleavages politically significant.

As noted earlier, there are strong decentralizing tendencies within the political centers of the underdeveloped states. The stability of any central coalition rests upon the various elites' perception that their participation in the coalition is yielding rewards; on their ability to maintain control over their own individual followings; and, where elements of patrimonialism are present, on the ability of the patrimonial leader to keep his personal retainers from entrenching themselves and establishing their own political fiefdoms.[14] The obvious difficulties in meeting these conditions explain much of the factional conflict that often appears in underdeveloped states.

Decentralization is particularly visible in areas such as northern Nigeria, Sierra Leone, and Ceylon, where traditional elites played a considerable role in the organization of the political center. In northern Nigeria, the Northern People's Congress

80 THE POLITICS OF INSTABILITY

"reflected and acknowledged the traditional identities of emirates as quasi-sovereign 'autonomous' states."[15] Executive bodies of the NPC, rather than establishing themselves as a higher authority to whose decisions the emirates were subject, showed themselves to be concerned merely with matters of common interest.[16] Even in countries such as Tanzania, where the leadership has tended to be more modernized, decentralizing pressures are present. Government ministries as well as personal followings can become the basis for private patrimonies.

> The leaders of government are themselves TANU leaders, deriving their authority in part from having been leaders of the independence movement, but also from being the inheritors of the colonial rulers. They ascend to the control of government machinery, receive salaries appropriate to their status, and monopolize the symbols of power—State House, large automobiles, titles. It is very important that they are the first inheritors. Since the new leaders moved into what is the first attempt at indigenous rule over the whole territory, *they have more scope to monopolize symbols and more freedom to try to create new institutions in their own image* . . . .[17]

In both northern Nigeria and Tanzania, efforts to promote centralization through the development of strong central party staffs were discouraged by the elected political elites themselves.[18] This almost natural pattern of decentralization is exacerbated in a variety of ways. First, the central leadership frequently attempts to gain control over both the center and the periphery by expanding the government's scope through the organization of development agencies and the integration of voluntary associations directly into the government. By offering the elites new sources of patrimony, the new agencies increase both the complexity of the coalitions and the possibility of competition between elites.

This decentralization pattern became particularly apparent in Ghana after 1960. The CPP—in reaction to a decline in its popularity, growing dissatisfaction among secondary and tertiary activists (who led the voluntary associations), and a general malaise in the party—was overhauled by Nkrumah and the CPP general secretary, Tawia Adamafio. Affiliated voluntary associations—the Trade Union Congress, the United Ghana Farmers' Council, the National Council of Ghana Women, the Ghana Young Pioneers, and the Cooperative Movement—were converted into CPP wings (and, therefore, quasi-government agencies). The demands of the various associations' leaders for party posts were satisfied, and, in theory, the organizational and ideological reach of the party was extended.[19] A new party vanguard was constructed, focused around the National Association of Socialist Students Organizations (NASSO) and the Kwame Nkrumah Ideological Institute. All of these groups soon emerged as competitors for dominance within the CPP and the Ghanaian political system. Even before this development, agencies such as the Cocoa Purchasing Co., Ltd., had become financial and patronage tools, not only for the CPP but also for the particular elites who ran them.[20]

Government enterprises have also played an especially visible role in Thailand. Most public enterprises and development agencies have been controlled by one or another personal clique and have been used to support and expand the various factions.[21] According to T. H. Silcock, banks have also been widely used as means of patrimony-building, with particular banks being controlled by the various factions and being utilized to provide credits, jobs, and business to faction members.[22]

Second, decentralization has also been exacerbated by political leadership that has proven, more often than not, to be less than competent. Ideological rigidity and limited understanding have caused many rulers of underdeveloped states to fritter "away their small initial political capital of legitimacy, distributive capacity, inertia, and coercion by investing it in nonessential undertakings. . . ."[23] More than this, a patrimonial leader's efforts to maintain his autonomy and authority seem, at times, self-defeating. Nkrumah's attempts to play party factions off against one another increasingly undermined his credibility with those factions, leaving him an "increasingly

THE POLITICS OF INSTABILITY

frightened and isolated leader presiding over a stagnating political machine."[24] By 1963, "Nkrumah had vanquished all his enemies, but he clearly had very few friends."[25]

The consequence of such incompetent leadership and rapid expansion of government activity is usually an escalation in factional conflict. Anxious to maintain their followings but confronted with limited resources at the center, elites utilize a variety of different resources for their own personal ends. Reciprocity between elites breaks down, and each seeks to mobilize resources on his own behalf rather than on behalf of a ruling coalition or patrimonial leader. Nation-building becomes, instead, faction-building.

Factional conflict can sometimes be ideological in origin. The 1958 dispute between Milton Margai and Albert Margai in the ruling Sierra Leone People's Party—which culminated in the latter's organizing an opposition party—was based, in large part, on the desire of Albert Margai and his supporters to speed social reform.[26] The split in the People's Action Party in Singapore was similarly ideological in its division between Communist and non-Communist groups.[27] The 1969 split in the Indian Congress Party High Command also reflected ideological differences.

More generally, however, factional conflict seems to have its genesis in personal conflicts among the elites and in their efforts to consolidate their own personal support. Faction-building focuses around the development of personal machines through which a particular leader can attract supporters. For the most part, such machines are dependent on the leader's continued access to patronage and government largess. Because they need such access, factional leaders tend to stay within the government unless they enjoy enough traditional status or personal wealth to maintain a following or unless they perceive the possibility of oppositional elites actually capturing control of the government (and its patronage).[28] In general, factional conflict remains within the confines of the regime, with conflicting elites utilizing their control over ministries and party organs to provide spoils to their existing supporters and to attract new ones.

Corruption, it should be noted, is an integral part of this process. Elites manipulate revenues to their own advantage and to the advantage of their supporters.[29]

In personal machine-building, communal, radical, and other such appeals are often "overtones" to an essentially personal conflict and provide disputing elites with additional means to attract supporters and consolidate their followings. In Ceylon, factionalism first manifested itself over policy disputes between S. W. R. D. Bandaranaike and the rest of the United Nationalist Party and, perhaps more important, over Bandaranaike's unsuccessful effort to be designated heir apparent to the prime minister. Bandaranaike ultimately broke with the UNP and joined the opposition. Even before the break, Bandaranaike had begun to meld personal contacts, local social networks, and mass support into a faction by utilizing his own personal wealth, his position as president of the All-Ceylon Village Committees Conference, his leadership of the communal *Sinhala Maha Sabha*, and his appeals for cultural, religious, and linguistic revivalism.[30]

The distinction between the process by which the center is expanded and faction-building is amorphous. The two are, in effect, one and the same. Expansion of center-periphery linkages, as we have noted, is indirect, dependent on personal linkages between a particular elite and his following. Whether such linkages provide support for the center (the formal seat of authority), or merely for the particular leader himself (a faction), is dependent on the patrimonial leader's often intangible ability to maintain his influence over his immediate followers (who have followings in their own right) and on the center's capability to provide the elites with material benefits for them and their followings. Factionalism, in other words, results not so much from the *development* of segmentation—segmentation is already present—as it does from the *collapse* of integrative relationships between the various elites themselves.

The consequences of intra-elite conflict for the rest of the political system are not readily predictable. The intermittent ties between the center and the periphery and within the

THE POLITICS OF INSTABILITY

periphery itself tend to allow these levels of political activity to exist as separate political arenas—each with its own unique conflicts, issues, and personalities. Factionalism in one level may or may not have consequences at another level. In India, intra-elite conflict in the center has frequently had only marginal impact on the political system as a whole. The defection of Acharya Kripalani from the Congress in 1951, following his defeat as a candidate for the Congress presidency, was not replicated to any real degree elsewhere in the party—even by those ideologically close to Kripalani.

At times, the political arenas—and the factions—are interlinked by common personalities. In Kenya, for example, the personal conflict between Oginga Odinga and Tom Mboya—which led to Odinga's defection from KANU in 1966—had ramifications for the lower levels of the party only in those districts where Odinga had an active personal following. In Central Nyanza district, Odinga's homeground, Odinga and his supporters dominated the KANU branch and, following Odinga's defection, converted *en masse* into a new party.[31] The Congress Party split in India in 1969 shows similar linkage patterns. The Syndicate group (Congress Organization) in the center controlled the Congress governments in the states of Mysore and Gujarat principally because of the personal influence of several Syndicate members in those states. Elsewhere in both Kenya and India, linkages between dissident factions at the various levels were relatively weak alliances of convenience; factions at lower levels allied themselves with a central faction less because of personal or ideological support for Odinga or the Syndicate than because their local factional opponent was linked to the other side. Such factional chains are, as a result, often composed of quite dissimilar elements and tend to be relatively instable. Again, the factions do not so much come into being (the segments comprising the factional chain already exist) as they jell at a particular moment in time.[32]

Ideological links between factions at various levels can, of course, occur. The Nationalist Association of Socialist Students Organizations in Ghana appears to have been such an ideologi-

85

cal faction, appearing at various levels of the party. Martin Staniland, in his study of the Ivory Coast, has suggested the existence of a "developmental faction," whose members "are identifiable by their claim that the modern 'rational' values they represent constitute the true interest of development and therefore entitle them (by virtue of their education or administrative training) to participate in politics" at the *sous-section* (intermediate government and party) level. Such groups can, at times, be mobilized by a central elite whose dissidence is, in part, ideological. Such factions, however, tend to be transitory. As Staniland has noted: "Perhaps this category should be described as a psychological collation rather than as a faction, as a presence rather than as a group."[33]

Opposition is an intricate part of this factional process, keyed, in a sense, by the fates of alliances, coalitions, and mergers within the government group. Opposition parties frequently have their genesis in factionalism within the elite, as the Kenyan example illustrates. Writing of India, Rajni Kothari has commented:

> Political dissent was thus a function of fragmentation of the political center of society rather than a projection of autonomous interests in the social and economic spheres. . . . It was not from the diversity of social interests but the fragmentation of political groups themselves that oppositional activity found its stimulus.
>
> Such an observation on the *process of dissent* also throws light on another peculiarity of Indian politics: the vague and overlapping differentiations between government, dissident factions within the government party, opposition parties, and dissident factions within the opposition parties.[34]

Such amorphousness is not unique to India.

As with its analysis of political institutions in general, current scholarship tends to reify the nature of political opposition, especially the opposition party. Political parties, in general, are seen as "discrete organizational entities, apart from governmental institutions, and operating on the basis of articulated 'support

THE POLITICS OF INSTABILITY

structures' and 'identities.' They are conceived as simply part of the representative structure of parliamentary government, contesting votes and seats, articulating and aggregating prevailing divisions in society, as part of the input processes of modern politics."[35] Perceived as such, opposition parties are associated almost entirely with the representation of social groups and interests unrepresented by the ruling party. Perceived in this way, opposition parties and government parties have no real structural differences. Both are discrete organizations primarily concerned with the articulation of specific social interests.

In reality, however, the cleavages that give rise to opposition are often personal ones among the elites. Opposition parties, lacking access to patronage and other government resources, are often structurally far less organized than the government party. As we have emphasized, it is control of and access to government that structures the loose coalition of elites and groups. Dissidence often severs that link to government, and factions which become opposition parties often either lose support or never succeed in expanding beyond the original dissident group of elites.

This is not to suggest that opposition groups have no social basis (ethnic, class, etc.). Opposition groups have been generated by social groups—regional, ethnic, linguistic, class—challenging the authority of the ruling elites. The NLM in Ghana is a classic example of such a party, as are the Tamil parties in Ceylon. Some opposition parties draw on a different ideological tradition and thus have been, in a sense, oppositional all along.[36] Even where the opposition party originated in an elite factional dispute, the party may—as a result of the appeals utilized by the dissident leaders—attract a different spectrum of social support. Angela Berger, in her study of opposition parties in the Indian state of Uttar Pradesh, has suggested that these parties eventually tended to attract the support of social groups which were mobilized after those linked to the government party and which, as a result, found access to the ruling party closed to them.[37] In Sierra Leone, the opposition PNP, organized by Albert Margai and led by a set of elites not dissimilar from those of the ruling party, succeeded in mobilizing considerable mass support.

Intra-elite conflict and social dissidence may, in effect, feed on one another. The rural rebellion in Morocco in 1958 was, in part, the result of the Rif tribesmen's feeling that the government had inadequately rewarded them for their contribution to the independence struggle and, in part, the result of the monarchy's conflicts with the Istiqlal elite.[38] Trying to create a counterbalance to the Istiqlal, the monarchy encouraged Ahardane, a political leader with strong ties in the area, to develop his own political party vis-à-vis the Istiqlal. That party's demand for official recognition by the Istiqlal government was part of the motive for the uprising.[39]

Opposition groups, in other words, frequently represent a nexus of dissident elites in the center, their immediate followings, and—because of their discontent or of the nature of the dissident elites' appeals—diverse elites and groups in the periphery. Such groupings are, not surprisingly, often weak and transitory. Social groups that have undergone mobilization relatively late tend to be isolated from one another and frequently share little beyond the common denominator of being denied access to the ruling party. Policy and ideological differences between the various elements of the opposition party may be greater than those between the dissident elites and those remaining in the government party. Dissident elites' efforts to mobilize support through appeals to primordial sentiment can ultimately be divisive where oppositions are amalgams of primordial groups. Finally, the lack of resources to meld together the various segments makes opposition parties vulnerable to penetration by the ruling elites. The segmentary character of the political process in the underdeveloped states defines the nature of opposition as well as that of rule.

The Politics of Communalism

Given the emphasis on the role of ethnicity in the politics of underdeveloped states, it is not surprising that the nature and boundaries of the various ethnic units are often perceived as relatively well defined, as "givens" with which one can begin an analysis of political behavior in these states.[40] The cleavages of kinship, language, race, and religion are divisions to be bridged. The massiveness of that task is a product of the particular intractability of such primordial divisions. Viewed in this light, the national political systems of the underdeveloped states become similar to the international political system, with its relatively clearly defined actors. As Donald Rothchild has put it:

> Because the social and cultural cleavages within new states are often so fundamental in nature, their domestic inter-group relations bear some resemblance to the type of political process appearing in the international order.[41]

This theoretical perspective offers no answer as to why one particular division in a society is politically more significant than another. As a result the analysis of communalism and the larger problem of national integration tends to focus around check lists of all possible social cleavages in a particular state.[42] Even more important, this viewpoint tends to endow a particular social conflict, and the particular groups in conflict, with an historic inevitability that may not be justified.

Changing social patterns in urban and rural areas of underdeveloped states have greatly modified the ways in which individuals identify themselves and their groups. In India, where traditionally the location of caste has been a village or group of villages, caste has gained wider geographical meaning.[43] Improved means of communication, Western education, and new economic opportunities have enabled the local castes (or subcastes, as they are more commonly called) to link up in geographically extended associations.[44] In towns, ethnic identities may be either reinforced or altered. Immigrants sharing a common origin may cluster together in one particular area and develop a sense of common identity which goes far beyond that of any earlier, rural community.[45] Elsewhere, identity is reformulated in response to the new urban environment. A man can be detribalized when he comes to live in the city and then "supertribalized" in terms of a new urban tribal identity.[46] In his study of an urban community in the copper belt of Northern Rhodesia, Arnold Epstein has noted that men from various ethnic groups in Nyasaland (Malawi) were all regarded as "Nyasalanders"—and they began to regard themselves as such.[47]

Administrative devices, such as censuses, can also affect identity. The British use of the classical Hindu fourfold classification of caste (varna)—Brahman, Kshatriya, Vaishya, Sudra—provided an impetus for many caste associations.[48] When educated caste elites began to seek recognition of higher status for their particular castes and subcastes, they soon discovered the need for regional subcaste organizations in order to secure uniformity in caste claims.[49]

Even when it is recognized that modernization and administrative decisions can alter and indeed create ethnic identity, the essential problem remains: how does a particular identity or set of identities become politically salient at a given point in time? In India, caste-derived sentiment has led to the emergence of a variety of political actors: caste associations, linking geographically dispersed members of similar subcastes (jatis); caste federations, linking several distinct endogamous castes into a single organization; sectarian religious-political movements; and communal organizations, articulating interests defined in terms of broad religious communities rather than in terms of caste.[50]

Political actors are generally viewed as being derivative from divisions within the society. In practice, the relationship is less explicit. Political leaders possess considerable freedom to choose whether or not they wish to depend on any social constituency and which constituency this will be. Interest groups, even those that are ostensibly communal, are seldom simply political expressions of explicit social groups. Rather, the interest group's definition of its own interests and its organizational framework tend to be strongly influenced by conflicts within the political system. Social groups and their interests are vaguely defined, and it is only in response to political con-

90   THE POLITICS OF INSTABILITY

flicts—between elites and between groups themselves—that interests become explicit and articulate. The critical variables in this process seem to be conflicts between the elites for political power and authority and their interaction with the patterns of social mobilization that begin to sharpen differences between ethnic communities.[51] As elite cohesion declines or disintegrates altogether, the elites are forced to seek new sources of support and new means of retaining their followings. In this situation, appeals to primordial sentiment are almost inevitable. Communalism, like opposition, is often inseparable from intra-elite conflict and factionalism. Thus, as Richard Sklar has suggested:

> It is less frequently recognized that tribal movements may be created and instigated to action by the new men of power in furtherance of their own special interests. . . .[52]

In India, dissident Congress elites have frequently utilized appeals of caste, tribe, region, and language in their efforts to generate new bases of political support, often using the relatively small but numerous caste, language, and cultural associations as organizational bases for such efforts.[53] In Sierra Leone, the organizer of the PNP, who was a former leader of the SLPP, split from a coalition of those two parties for largely personal reasons and organized yet another party which, because of his appeals, had a strongly communal orientation.[54]

Multiple permutations of communal political activity appear to be possible, depending on the nature of the elite conflict, the degree of development within a particular community, the degree to which a community is segregated from other communities, and the degree to which existing leader-following linkages are encapsulated in one ethnic group as opposed to spanning across several.

In societies where elites and their followings are confined to particular communities, communal appeals are overtones to existing patron-client, kinship, and personal relationships. The mixture of communal appeals with existing social structures can endow a community with considerable internal cohesion, but it can also make intercommunal cohesion or national integration more difficult. Writing of Malaysia, Burma, and Laos, Scott has noted:

> Except at the apex of the political structure where a leader may have leaders of smaller communal groups as his clients, most patrons have followings that are almost exclusively drawn from their own communities. Intercommunal integration tends to take place near the apex of the political structure with the base of each communal pyramid remaining largely separate.[55]

Such intercommunal elite linkages are reminiscent of those discussed by Arend Lijphart in his analysis of the "consociational democracies" of Western Europe—polities which are characterized by mutually reinforcing cleavages and by the political elites' deliberate efforts to counteract the effects of cultural fragmentation.[56] Such integration "at the apex" is fragile. Lijphart, for example, argues that such interaction can be achieved and maintained only if (1) elites recognize its desirability; (2) subcultures are relatively encapsulated and isolated from one another; and (3) subcultures possess a high degree of internal political cohesion so that elites can make necessary compromises for coalition without loss of support. The last condition, in particular, is elusive. The increasing number of new patrons and the competition between elites to expand their personal machines can make cohesion within the community highly tenuous. In effect, the "short-circuiting" of elite-following linkages discussed previously undermines unity within the community. The community is incapable of presenting leaders who can negotiate at the apex without being challenged within their own following.[57] The lack of such leaders, particularly when elites canvass for support by appealing to primordial sentiment, makes for explosive possibilities. In Malaysia, the growing dissensus among the Malay political elite laid the basis for the communal explosions that occurred in May 1969.[58] A study of Hindu-Sikh communal rivalry in Punjab state in India reveals a similar process. The competition between elite

THE POLITICS OF INSTABILITY

groups within each community has made any long-term resolution of differences between the two communities tenuous at best.[59]

When elite-following linkages cross ethnic divisions, communal appeals by elites can be even more destabilizing. Commenting on the communal conflicts in Rwanda and Burundi, Lemarchand has argued:

> where cultural cleavages not only are prominent but tend to coincide with patron and clients, these cleavages may help break up the patron-client nexus. Thus, the greater the cultural differences between patrons and clients, and the more conspicuous the social distance between them, the greater the likelihood of violent ethnic strife in conditions of rapid social mobilization.[60]

What I mean to suggest is that communal conflict is not inevitable in plural societies. If it must be accepted that social mobilization, by engendering competition between groups, tends to cause those groups to define that competition in communal terms and that differential mobilization further sharpens group differences by multiplying coincident social cleavages,[61] it must also be recognized that communal cleavage is often no better defined than class or regional cleavage. Traditional identity is defined in terms of local bonds. A communal identity is not traditional in this sense and is vulnerable to considerable changes in its inclusiveness.

Communalism, as a result, tends to be a specific political orientation, a response to a particular set of issues and personalities in a particular context.[62] As one study has argued: "Every actor in the political community, no matter how unimportant, has a multiplicity of potential foci of social solidarity. The appropriate role is prescribed by the nature of the situation—or more precisely, by the actor's perception of the situation."[63] What needs to be emphasized, however, is that the "actor's perception of the situation" is not happenstance. More often than not, it is structured by the nature of the political elites' appeals. In Nigeria, despite the success of a "class"

93

general strike in Lagos, Ibadan, and other important cities in 1964, parliamentary elections held several months later saw those same trade unionists reject trade union leaders as political candidates and vote for communal party candidates.[64] The lines of political cleavage did not, however, redraw themselves so much as they were redrawn by the competing political elites who reactivated the political salience of ethnic clan unions and personal networks.[65]

Communalism, to summarize this brief analysis, is not a lingering vestige of the past, comprehensible in terms of traditional political behavior. Rather, it is inseparable from the political process of the underdeveloped state as a whole, defined by the personalism of elite interaction and feuding as well as by the segmentation of the society. Communalism is only one characteristic of a shift from elite cohesion to elite dissensus.

Elite Dissensus and the Military Coup d'Etat

The instability of the underdeveloped state has come to be increasingly associated with the incursion of military elites and organizations into the politics of those states. The most obvious example, of course, is the *coup d'état*. The coups themselves, however, have long since been outnumbered by scholarly efforts to explain them. The occurrence of coups has been linked to breakdowns in economic development and to economic stagnation,[66] to the failure of political institutions,[67] to cultural variables,[68] to professionalism and militant nationalism within the military itself,[69] to lack of professionalism and the emergence of the military as an adjunct to one or more social groups,[70] and to proximity to other military coups.[71] These explanations have, in fact, been linked together to generate a more or less summary explanation. As one scholar has summarized the argument:

modernization produces disorientation or conflict of values in traditional societies, it leaves power vacuums, econom-

THE POLITICS OF INSTABILITY

ic maladjustments, and dysfunctional stratifications with which the incumbent politicians cannot cope. The result is disequilibrium and uneven development, a situation presenting the military with the opportunity to intervene. There then occurs an expansion of the role of the military. "The army intervenes because other elites are absent, impotent or indifferent; it improvises and expands its role to carry the burden created by a modernization crisis."[72]

These hypotheses have proven to be largely unsatisfactory. In the first place, the plethora of coups in countries of virtually every combination of social, economic, and political situation seems to make the incidence of coups almost random, independent of any of the variables suggested.[73]

Second, these explanations tend to distort the nature of the military itself in the underdeveloped state. The general analysis of military intervention is similar to that concerning the emergence of the dominant nationalist parties discussed in Chapter 2. Just as it was argued that such parties represent superiority in organization vis-à-vis their competitors, so it is argued that the military enjoys organizational superiority vis-à-vis all other social and political organizations. The military, goes the argument, is a "heavy" institution and dominant because of that heaviness. With some notable exceptions, however, this is not the case. In Africa, especially, the militaries have usually been small and poorly trained. The army, "far from being a model of hierarchical organization" and potentially dominant on the sheer basis of that organization, "tends to be an assemblage of armed men who may or may not obey their officers."[74]

Finally, all of these explanations tend—despite efforts to overcome a Western repugnance to political action by the military—to view the military as an actor whose role is normally outside of the political process. Whether intervention is the result of factors internal to the military (professionalism or the lack of it) or external to the military (economic stagnation, political decay), the circumstances represent an aberration from what ought to prevail. That the aberrant circumstances are increasingly the norm is, of course, recognized by most scholars.

95

Nonetheless, the bias persists and, to a considerable degree, influences the analysis. Coups are invariably explained by reference to an abnormal event or series of events.

Such explanations tend to overstate the institutional stability and cohesion in the new states. The political center, whether organized around a patrimonial leader or a coalition of elites, exhibits little such stability and little legitimacy in the common usage of the term. There has been, in other words, precious little authority or legitimacy to be undermined. Military involvement has flowed from the very nature of the underdeveloped political process itself, not from extraordinary circumstances.

In many states, the military elites were involved in politics almost from the beginning. In states such as Burma, Indonesia, and Algeria, the military played a role in the independence movement, and after independence its role was expanded as military elites became active participants in the political process. These military elites, regardless of their professionalism, were political elites as well. In other states, military elites were involved in the political process as political elites sought to expand their patrimonies to include the armies or parts of armies. In Ghana, for example, Nkrumah sought to expand patrimonial control over the military in a variety of ways: creating a personal palace guard from out of the regular military and police, establishing a military intelligence unit to monitor the army, and placing officers he personally trusted in command positions.[75] In Pakistan, President Iskander Mirza attempted to consolidate his control over the system by naming a man he thought amenable to his influence, General Ayub Khan, to be Commander-in-Chief and Minister of Defence.[76]

In some states, the military and military elites were not involved directly in the political process as much as they were enlisted—or, at least, were the target of an effort to enlist them—into what was, or was to be, a patrimonial army for one or more of the political elites. In Pakistan, for example, when Mirza declared martial law and invited General Ayub to be Chief Martial Law Administrator, Mirza clearly intended this strategy to coerce his opposition. Instead, Ayub displaced Mirza as well.[77] In Dahomey, Ahomadegbe's efforts to put down trade union strikes with the military had a similar consequence.[78] In Uganda, Milton Obote successfully utilized the military in May 1966 to resolve a long-festering conflict between the kingdom of Buganda and the Uganda central government. All such efforts —successful or not—tend to enhance considerably the role of the military. As one scholar has stated:

> When a shift from power to force occurs, it is accompanied by a shift in the relative "market value" of existing structures: in the case of the new African states, the value of political parties and of civilian administration has undergone a sort of deflation, while the value of the police and of the military has been vastly increased.[79]

"Specialists on violence" gain primacy over "specialists on symbols," to use phrases suggested by Robert C. North.[80] This has been true even in places like Upper Volta, Somalia, Burma, and Turkey, where the military has not been overtly sought as a tool but where armed clashes, riots, strikes, insurgencies—all related to intra-elite conflict—have become rampant.[81] In effect, the personal factionalism that characterizes the political system embroils the military, either in the process of faction-building or as a result of the intensifying conflict generated by that faction-building.

The military's involvement in the political process of the underdeveloped states is not the intervention of an external institution into the political system as much as it is embroilment of a particular set of military elites because of the very expanding nature of factional conflict. Embroilment in the political system—especially a system in which armed conflict has developed—makes the military elites' dominance probable simply because of their control over coercive capability. In Indonesia, the Communist-led coup of September 30, 1965 against the military, which saw the assassination of six senior military officers, was quickly broken by a crushing counterblow mounted by Generals Suharto, Nasution, and other senior army

97

commanders. In the final analysis, control over strategic coercive capability determines who rules.

Coercive capability need not, it should be stressed, be massive. The tenuousness of elite coalitions in the political center and the instability of linkages between center and periphery make the political center highly vulnerable to limited amounts of coercive capacity. Zolberg has noted that the two smallest African armies at the time of their interventions, the Togolese army of 250 men in 1963 and the Central African Republic's army of 600 men in 1966, were easily successful.[82] In South Korea, the actual coup forces were small (3,500 men was the estimate); the rest of the military was initially hostile to the coup or neutral. The coup's success in quickly taking Seoul increasingly brought much of the rest of the army over to the side of the elites involved in the coup. Similarly, a regime's control over a strategically placed military unit is likely to forestall a coup regardless of the factional conflict and disorder. In Senegal, Senghor countered Mamadou Dia's deployment of the gendarmerie through his control over a single battalion of airborne troops.[83]

There are, to be sure, an almost infinite number of factors that could comprise a coup situation. Estrangement between military and political elites, a growing sense of nationalism on the part of the military, the emergence of corporate interests in the military, the fragmentation of the military in warring ethnic groups are only several. In essence, recent experience demonstrates that in an underdeveloped political system a coup is likely to occur in almost any kind of conflict situation. Specific features of a country determine the timing, the actors, and the demands. What underdeveloped political systems have in common is the endemic character of factional conflict and the expansive nature of that conflict. What military elites a conflict will embroil is not really predictable. Undeniably, military elites are likely to be involved ultimately, and, in a climate of escalating forceful conflict, such elites enjoy an almost natural superiority.

The political process in underdeveloped states is a paradoxical one. The bases of consolidation in such states—patrimonialism and material incentive—provide the sources of decentralization as well. The limited durability of patrimonial authority and the continued dearth of material incentives seem to make factionalism and disintegrative behavior almost inevitable. To return to the concluding statement of the previous chapter, the political process appears to be hostile to the very process of institutionalization. Not only are the personal linkages between center and periphery erratic, but the political elites' efforts to establish their own political fiefdoms—through personal factions, dominance of party wings, or control of ministries—militates against stabilized procedures and organizations through which consolidation might be achieved. In such an environment, conflict—factional, communal, oppositional, armed—becomes the norm rather than an aberration. Rather than being the consequence of breakdowns or political decay, the politics of instability is inherent in the segmentary political process itself.

NOTES

1. Aristide Zolberg, "The Structure of Political Conflict in the New States of Tropical Africa," *American Political Science Review*, LXII, 1 (1968), 70.
2. *Ibid.*, p. 71.
3. S. N. Eisenstadt, "Social Change and Modernization in African Societies South of the Sahara," *Cahiers d'Etudes Africaines*, V, 3 (1965), 453-471.
4. Samuel Huntington, *Political Order in Changing Societies* (New Haven: Yale University Press, 1968), p. 5.
5. Karl W. Deutsch, "Social Mobilization and Political Development," *American Political Review*, LV, 3 (1961), 498.
6. Zolberg, p. 76.
7. *Ibid.*, pp. 73-74.
8. Robert Melson and Howard Wolpe, "Modernization and the Politics of Communalism: A Theoretical Perspective," *American Political Science Review*, LXIV, 4 (1970), 1115.
9. Huntington, p. 55.
10. James O'Connell, "The Inevitability of Instability," *The Journal of Modern African Studies*, 5, 2 (1971), 188.

11. Conflict in segmentary societies is discussed in Lloyd Fallers, "Political Sociology and the Anthropological Study of African Politics," *Archives Européennes de Sociologie*, IV, 2 (1963), 311-329.

12. John Kautsky, *The Political Consequences of Modernization* (New York: John Wiley and Sons, 1972), pp. 139-142.

13. For two excellent studies of these cleavages, see Victor T. LeVine, *Political Leadership in Africa: Post-Independence Generational Conflict in Upper Volta, Senegal, Niger, Dahomey, the Central African Republic* (Stanford: Hoover Institution on War, Revolution and Peace, 1967); and William B. Quandt, *Revolution and Political Leadership: Algeria, 1954-1968* (Cambridge, Mass.: M.I.T. Press, 1969).

14. For examples of just how difficult it is for patrimonial leaders to accomplish this, see Henry Bienen, *Tanzania: Party Transformation and Economic Development* (Princeton: Princeton University Press, 1970), pp. 158-167, 185-195; and H. L. Bretton, *The Rise and Fall of Kwame Nkrumah* (London: Praeger, 1967).

15. C. S. Whitaker, *The Politics of Tradition* (Princeton: Princeton University Press, 1970), p. 365.

16. *Ibid.*

17. Bienen, p. 195.

18. *Ibid.*, pp. 196-197; Whitaker, p. 366.

19. Dennis L. Cohen, "The Convention People's Party of Ghana: Representational or Solidarity Party," *Canadian Journal of African Studies*, IV, 2 (1970), 178-179.

20. Government of Ghana, *Report of the Commission of Inquiry into the Affairs of the Cocoa Purchasing Company, Ltd.* (Accra: Government Printers, 1956).

21. Fred Riggs, *Thailand: The Modernization of a Bureaucratic Polity* (Honolulu: East-West Center Press, 1966), pp. 242-310.

22. T. H. Silcock, "Money and Banking," in T. H. Silcock, ed., *Thailand: Social and Economic Studies in Development* (Durham, N.C.: Duke University Press, 1967), pp. 183-185.

23. Zolberg, p. 72.

24. Barbara Callaway and Emily Card, "Political Constraints on Economic Development in Ghana," in Michael Lofchie, ed., *The State of the Nations: Constraints on Development in Independent Africa* (Berkeley and Los Angeles: University of California Press, 1971), p. 73.

25. David Apter, "Nkrumah, Charisma, and the Coup," *Daedalus*, XCVII, 3 (1968), 784.

26. John R. Cartwright, *Politics in Sierra Leone 1947-1967* (Toronto: University of Toronto Press, 1970), p. 109. Even here, however, there were other dimensions to the factionalism. The dissident group was slightly younger and better educated, for example.

27. Thomas J. Bellows, *The People's Action Party of Singapore: Emergence of a Dominant Party System*, Monograph Series No. 14 (New Haven: Yale University Southeast Asia Studies, 1970), pp. 35-44.

28. This last factor played a critical role in the defections from the Congress Party in India after 1967.

29. James C. Scott argues that such corruption has its benefits in that the competition to attract supporters makes the masses the beneficiaries of the corruption. See his "An Essay on the Political Functions of Corruption," *Asian Studies*, V, 3 (1967), 501-523.

30. See Calvin Woodward, *The Growth of a Party System in Ceylon* (Providence: Brown University Press, 1969), pp. 76-79; and Robert N. Kearney, *Communalism and Language in the Politics of Ceylon* (Durham, N.C.: Duke University Press, 1967), pp. 63-67.

31. On Kenya and the 1966 elections, see Cherry Gertzel, *The Politics of Independent Kenya, 1963-1968* (Evanston, Ill.: Northwestern University Press, 1970).

32. The literature on factional conflict in India includes virtually all studies of Indian politics. See, in particular, Paul Brass, *Factional Politics in an Indian State* (Berkeley and Los Angeles: University of California Press, 1969); Richard Sisson, *The Congress Party in Rajasthan* (Berkeley and Los Angeles: University of California Press, 1972); Myron Weiner, *State Politics in India* (Princeton: Princeton University Press, 1968); and Iqbal Narain, *State Politics in India* (Meerut, India: Meinakshi Prakashan, 1957).

33. Martin Staniland, "Single-Party Regimes and Political Change: The P.D.C.I. and Ivory Coast Politics," in Colin Leys, ed., *Politics and Change in Developing Countries* (Cambridge, Eng.: Cambridge University Press, 1969), p. 173.

34. Rajni Kothari, *Politics in India* (Boston: Little, Brown and Company, 1970), p. 161.

35. *Ibid.*, p. 159.

36. See, for example, Gerald A. Heeger, "Discipline vs. Mobilization: Party Building and the Punjab Jana Sangh," *Asian Survey*, XII, 10 (1972), 864-878.

37. Angela Berger, *Opposition in a Dominant-Party System* (Berkeley and Los Angeles: University of California Press, 1969).

38. On the rural rebellions in Morocco and their relationship to intra-elite conflict, see Ernest Gellner, "Patterns of Rural Rebellion in Morocco: Tribes as Minorities," *Archives Européennes de Sociologie*, III, 2 (1962), 297-311; Ernest Gellner, "Tribalism and Social Change in North Africa," in W. H. Lewis, ed., *French-Speaking Africa: the Search for Identity* (New York: Walker, 1965), pp. 107-118; and W. H. Lewis, "Feuding and Social Change in Morocco," *Journal of Conflict Resolution*, V (1961), 43-54.

39. Gellner, p. 116.

40. See, for example, Geertz, pp. 105-157. Geertz defines national integration as "the aggregation of independently defined, specifically outlined traditional primordial groups into larger, more diffused units, whose implicit frame of reference is not the local scene but the 'nation' . . ." (p. 163); he notes, "By a primordial sentiment

is meant one that stems from the 'givens'—or, more precisely, as culture is inevitably involved in such matters, the assumed 'givens' of social existence" (p. 109).

41. Donald Rothchild, "Ethnicity and Conflict Resolution," *World Politics*, XXII, 4 (1970), 597.

42. Geertz, pp. 112-113; Emerson, *From Empire to Nation*, chapters 6, 7, 8. Similar types of check lists with regard to developed nations can be found in Seymour Martin Lipset and Stein Rokkan, eds., *Party Systems and Voter Alignments* (New York: Free Press, 1967); and Richard Rose and Derek Urwin, "Social Cohesion, Political Parties, and Strains in Regimes," *Comparative Politics*, V, 1 (1969), 7-67.

43. Lloyd I. Rudolph and Susanne Hoeber Rudolph, *The Modernity of Tradition* (Chicago: University of Chicago Press, 1967), p. 30.

44. *Ibid.*, p. 31.

45. On this phenomenon, see May Edel, "African Tribalism: Some Reflections on Uganda," *Political Science Quarterly*, LXXX, 3 (1965), 357-72.

46. Immanuel Wallerstein, "Ethnicity and National Integration in West Africa," *Cahiers d'Etudes Africaines*, I, 3 (1960), 131.

47. Arnold L. Epstein, *Politics in an Urban African Community* (Manchester, Eng.: Manchester University Press, 1958), p. 236.

48. M. N. Srinivas, *Caste in Modern India and Other Essays* (Bombay: Asia Publishing House, 1962), p. 18. Rudolph and Rudolph, pp. 116-117, also discuss the role of the 1901 census in provoking social change in India.

49. A roughly similar phenomenon occurred in Uganda and the Congo. Administrative determinations were made as to which peoples belonged to which tribe, and ethnic identifications emerged around these administratively defined divisions. See Crawford Young, *Politics in the Congo* (Princeton, N.J.: Princeton University Press, 1965), pp. 245-246; and Nelson Kasfir, "Cultural Subnationalism in Uganda," in V. A. Olorunsola, ed., *The Politics of Cultural Subnationalism* (Garden City, N.Y.: Doubleday and Company, 1972), p. 61.

50. The literature on caste and caste in politics in India is extensive. For a theoretical discussion of the political consequences of caste mobilization in India, see Rudolph and Rudolph, pp. 15-154.

51. For a detailed argument as to the relationship between social mobilization and communalism, see Melson and Wolpe.

52. Richard Sklar, "Political Science and National Integration—A Radical Approach," *The Journal of Modern African Studies*, V, 1 (1967), 7.

53. For one such case, see Gerald A. Heeger, "Politics of Integration: Community, Party, and Integration in Punjab" (Ph.D. dissertation, University of Chicago, 1971). See also Jyotirindra Das Gupta, *Language Conflict and National Development* (Berkeley and Los Angeles: University of California Press, 1970), especially chapters VII and VIII.

54. Martin Kilson, *Political Change in a West African State* (Cambridge, Mass.: Harvard University Press, 1966), pp. 271-272.

55. James C. Scott, "Patron-Client Politics and Political Change in Southeast Asia," *American Political Science Review*, LXVI, 1 (1972), 105.

56. Arend Lijphart, "Consociational Democracy," *World Politics*, XXI, 2, (1969), 207-226. See also Arend Lijphart, *The Politics of Accommodation: Pluralism and Democracy in the Netherlands* (Berkeley and Los Angeles: University of California Press, 1968).

57. Cynthia H. Enloe, *Ethnic Conflict and Political Development* (Boston: Little, Brown and Company, 1973), pp. 169-170, makes a similar argument.

58. This event is summarized in *ibid.*, pp. 175-178. See also, Cynthia H. Enloe, *Multi-Ethnic Politics: The Case of Malaysia* (Berkeley: Center for South and Southeast Asia Studies, 1970); and K. J. Ratnam and R. S. Milne, "The 1969 Parliamentary Election in West Malaysia," *Pacific Affairs*, XLIII, 2 (1970), 203-226.

59. Heeger, "The Politics of Integration," especially pp. 264-331.

60. René Lemarchand, "Political Clientelism and Ethnicity in Tropical Africa: Competing Solidarities in Nation-Building," *American Political Science Review*, LXVI, 1 (1972), p. 84.

61. Melson and Wolpe, p. 1114.

62. This proposition reproduces that made by Melson and Wolpe (p. 1126) and draws on the works of Max Gluckman, "Tribalism in Modern British Central Africa," *Cahiers d'Etudes Africaines*, 1 (1960), 55-70; A. L. Epstein, *Politics in an Urban African Community* (Manchester, Eng.: Manchester University Press, 1958); and Clyde Mitchell, *The Kalela Dance* (Manchester, Eng.: Manchester University Press, 1956). All assert that the situation selects the identity. That is, ethnicity should be most important in social life, selection of marriage partner, etc., while class may be salient in economic matters, particularly those dealing with negotiations with, for example, factory owners.

63. Charles W. Anderson, Fred R. von der Mehden, and Crawford Young, *Issues of Political Development* (Englewood Cliffs, N.J.: Prentice-Hall, Inc., 1967), p. 60.

64. Robert Melson, "Ideology and Inconsistency: The Cross-Pressured Nigerian Worker," *American Political Science Review*, LXV, 1 (1971), 161-171.

65. For a discussion of these networks in Eastern Nigeria, see Audrey C. Smock, *Ibo Politics: The Role of Ethnic Unions in Eastern Nigeria* (Cambridge, Mass.: Harvard University Press, 1971).

66. See Mancur Olson, "Rapid Growth as a Destabilising Force," *Journal of Economic History*, XXIII (1963), 529-532; Robert D. Putnam, "Toward Explaining Military Intervention in Latin American Politics," *World Politics*, XX, 1 (October 1967), 83-110; and Martin Needler, "Political Development and Military Intervention in Latin America," *American Political Science Review*, LX (1966), 616-626.

67. This view is most associated with Samuel Huntington, pp.

142-263, and takes a variety of forms. The military itself may be stressed in terms of its modernity, its "heaviness" vis-à-vis other institutions. See, for example, Guy Pauker, "Southeast Asia as a Problem Area in the Next Decade," *World Politics*, XI, 3 (1959), 325-345; Lucian W. Pye, "Armies in the Process of Political Modernization," in John J. Johnson, ed., *The Role of the Military in Underdeveloped Countries* (Princeton: Princeton University Press, 1962); Morris Janowitz, *The Military in the Political Development of New Nations* (Chicago: University of Chicago Press, 1964); Marion J. Levy, Jr., *Modernization and the Structure of Societies*, Vol. II (Princeton: Princeton University Press, 1966), pp. 571-605; and Henry Bienen, "The Background to the Contemporary Study of Militaries and Modernization," in Henry Bienen, ed., *The Military and Modernization* (Chicago: Aldine-Atherton, 1971), pp. 1-34. In terms of the military's resultant role-expansion in the face of the inadequacy of civilian institutions, see, for example, Moshe Lissak, "Modernization and the Role Expansion of the Military in Developing Countries," *Comparative Studies in Society and History*, IX, 3 (1967), 233-255. The environment in which this "heavy" institution exists may be emphasized, e.g., the praetorian society where "all society forces are politicized." See Huntington; and Amos Perlmutter, "The Praetorian State and the Praetorian Army: Towards a Theory of Civil-Military Relations in Developing Countries," *Comparative Politics*, I, 3 (1969), 382-404.

68. See, especially, Samuel Finer, *The Man on Horseback* (New York: Frederick A. Praeger, 1962); and Merle Kling, "Violence and Politics in Latin America," in P. Halmos, ed., *Latin American Sociological Studies* (Sociological Review Monograph 11, 1967), pp. 119-131.

69. Fred von der Mehden and G. W. Anderson, "Political Action by the Military in Developing Areas," *Social Research*, XXVIII, 4 (1961), 459-480; Karl Hopkins, "Civil-Military Relations in Developing Countries," *British Journal of Sociology*, XVII, 2 (1966), 165-182; M. D. Feld, "Professionalism, Nationalism, and the Alienation of the Military," in Jacques van Doorn, ed., *Armed Forces and Society* (The Hague: Mouton and Co., 1966), pp. 55-70. Related to these is Robert M. Price, "A Theoretical Approach to Military Rule in the New States: Reference-Group Theory and the Ghanaian Case," *World Politics*, XXIII, 3 (1971), 399-430. Price, however, argues that professionalism in the Ghanaian army led military elites to identify with the British military and to intervene against Nkrumah when he challenged the British pattern and when he sought to establish supply linkages with Communist nations. Intervention, in this case, was the result of something akin to a "supranational careerism" rather than nationalism.

70. Samuel Huntington, *The Soldier and the State* (New York: Random House, 1957). More recently, the conditions under which a military's corporate or professional identity develops and breaks down have been subject to theorizing. See, especially, A. Stepan, *The Military in Politics: Changing Patterns of Civilian-Military Relationships in Brazil* (Princeton: Princeton University Press, 1971); René

Lemarchand, "Civilian-Military Relations in Former Belgian Africa: The Military as a Contextual Elite," paper delivered to American Political Science Association, 1972 Annual Meeting, Washington, D.C.; and Robin Luckham, *The Nigerian Military: A Sociological Analysis of Authority and Revolt, 1960-1967* (Cambridge, Eng.: Cambridge University Press, 1971).

71. Claude Welch, "The Roots and Implications of Military Intervention," in Claude Welch, Jr., ed., *Soldier and State in Africa* (Evanston, Ill.: Northwestern University Press, 1970), pp. 26-27.

72. Robert Dowse, "The Military and Political Development," in Leys, pp. 213-214. The quoted sentence is from Lissak (see footnote 67).

73. Zolberg, "The Structure of Political Conflict," p. 78.

74. *Ibid.*, p. 72.

75. Jon Kraus, "Political Change, Conflict, and Development in Ghana," in Philip Foster and Aristide R. Zolberg, eds., *Ghana and the Ivory Coast* (Chicago: University of Chicago Press, 1971), pp. 59-60.

76. On this attempt, see Mohammed Ayub Khan, *Friends, Not Masters: A Political Autobiography* (London: Oxford University Press, 1967).

77. *Ibid.*

78. W. A. E. Skurnik, "The Military and Politics: Dahomey and Upper Volta," in Welch, pp. 78-79.

79. Aristide Zolberg, "Military Intervention in the New States of Tropical Africa," in Henry Bienen, ed., *The Military Intervenes* (New York: Russell Sage Foundation, 1968), p. 80.

80. Robert C. North, "Chinese Communist and Kuomintary Elites," in Harold Lasswell and Daniel Lerner, eds., *World Revolutionary Elites* (Cambridge, Mass.: M.I.T. Press, 1965), pp. 319-455. 455.

81. On Somalia, see I. M. Lewis, "The Politics of the 1969 Somali Coup," *The Journal of Modern African Studies*, X, 3 (1972), 383-408.

82. Zolberg, "The Structure of Political Conflict," p. 79.

83. *Ibid.*

5

The Military in Power

T

he regimes constituted by military elites after their seizure of power have proved enigmatic to the scholar. The bold rhetoric at the installation of such regimes calls for national reconstruction and national unity and the indictment of the politicians whom the military leaders have replaced. As Joseph Mobutu declared:

> What could the army high command do? Only what it has done: sweep the politicians out. . . . Nothing counted for them [the politicians] but power . . . and what the exercise of power could bring them. Filling their pockets, exploiting the Congo and its inhabitants seemed to be their only purpose.[1]

To what extent is such rhetoric an indication of capability on the part of the new rulers? As Claude Welch was led to ask: "Can a military-based government cope more successfully with the difficulties civilian regimes encountered? Are some of these problems susceptible to solution by means congenial to the governing military junta, in ways that escaped the preceding civilian regime?"[2]

In the absence of extensive data on military governments, scholars have tended to vacillate with the ideological winds in their views of such regimes. The late 1950's and early 1960's were characterized by "tough-minded" liberals arguing that the

107

military, as an "industrial-type" social organization, was particularly fitted for modernizing underdeveloped societies.[3] More recently, however, has come a different perspective, one that questions the capability of the military to accomplish modernization goals. In this view, the military's particular kind of organization represents more of a barrier than a means to modernization.

> Vanguard, feet marching, ranks serried, battlements, charges, the great objective: the imagery is the familiar one of the proving ground and the infantry attack. Command and discipline, direction and momentum count for everything. . . . Surely, if the ills of the body politic could have been cured so easily, the occasion for a military coup would never have arisen. The political arena is not a defile. Civil servants cannot administer laws by advancing in serried ranks. Economic planners cannot augment production by charging battlements. . . . Above all, the objectives in politics are always in question. Any junta of field-grade officers that expects to reach a sacred but unspecified goal—and to reach it by storm in a few hours or even weeks—is in for an awakening. . . .[4]

Recent history, as Ann Ruth Willner has pointed out, illustrates the precariousness not only of these particular broad generalizations but of any generalizations about the increasingly diverse phenomena generally lumped together as "military regimes."[5] Yet, the questions raised by Claude Welch remain and, in fact, become more pressing as military regimes establish themselves as the norm rather than the exception in Africa and Asia. Despite the relative recentness of the military regime in the underdeveloped states and the continued scarcity of data about such regimes, some tentative answers to those questions must be attempted.

A starting point in the analysis of military regimes is the recognition that the armed forces as a whole seldom rule. The military regime is a government in which *particular* military elites rule. These elites may or may not have the support of the rest of the armed forces. Gaining and maintaining that support is, in fact, generally a continual concern to the ruling military elites. In this sense, then, the argument as to whether or not the particular type of social organization that the military represents is an effective means of political development is an argument about something that, more often than not, simply does not exist. The armed forces in the underdeveloped states—sometimes wholly undisciplined and frequently characterized by ethnic cleavages, hostility between the officers and ranks, and rifts within the officer corps themselves—have, with few exceptions, been far from well organized. Moreover, the cleavages within the military are often exacerbated after it seizes power and becomes further divided between those officers who assume positions in the government and those who do not.

Military elites, as was the case with their civilian predecessors, confront the segmented political systems that they seek to govern, not as leaders of highly disciplined, monolithic organizations, but rather as elites in search of (inevitably precarious) primacy. Political consolidation, far from being an accomplished fact brought about by the imposition of a military hierarchy on society, remains the principal, if elusive, goal.

Unlike their civilian predecessors, however, the military rulers seem to share a common perception of political consolidation that is curiously antipolitical. Openly hostile to politicians, suspicious of mass participation, distrustful, in fact, of politics in general, the military rulers have sought to create an "apolitical calm, undisturbed by the erratic movements of partisan bodies."[6] Their efforts have been unsuccessful. Yet, recent events suggest that the distrust of politics makes the military regime a potentially self-contradictory regime, one in which, despite the military elites' concern for centralizing authority, decentralizing "pulls" are more assertive than ever.

Antipolitics

There are striking similarities in the ways in which military rulers articulate their perceptions of the problems they con-

109

front. Ruling military elites exhibit a deep distrust of social conflict in general and of any political process that recognizes such conflict as legitimate. As Zolberg has stated:

> They conceive of national unity as "oneness," defined negatively by the absence of social conflict stemming from regionalism, primordial loyalties such as ethnicity or religious affiliations. In all countries, "ethnic particularism" has been condemned and its manifestations through voluntary associations prohibited. The goal seems to be the achievement of homogeneity by political fiat, as if the rulers genuinely believed that the absence of conflict somehow produces national integration.[7]

These attitudes have frequently been called "nonpolitical"; and it has been argued that they were shared by many leaders of African one-party states.[8] But there are crucial differences between the views of military elites and those of such civilian leaders. The military elites appear to be less nonpolitical than overtly antipolitical. For the leaders of one-party states, such as Nkrumah and Touré, unanimity was to be achieved by the encouragement of mass participation. As long as the mobilization process was controlled by a single group of elites, mobilization and participation were the principal means of communicating new normative goals and a new political vocabulary. Mobilization and participation served to jar men out of their parochialism. The military rulers, in contrast, appear to distrust not simply pluralistic participation but participation *per se*. All participation, in their view, is inevitably pluralistic and, therefore, inevitably divisive. The masses, manipulated by politicians, are forever falling prey to "clanism, factionalism, and consciousness of family background."[9]

Not surprisingly, military regimes have usually sharply curtailed political activities. They generally banned political parties—even those that had opposed the regime ousted by the military. In Pakistan and South Korea, substantial numbers of politicians were barred from public activity altogether.[10] In Nigeria, the military regime went so far as to dismiss all elected officials as far down as the level of local politicians.[11] Because they were seen to engender particularism, regional jurisdictions were often altered. In the Congo, General Mobutu amalgamated the twenty-two provinces into twelve. In Nigeria, following the coup of January 1966, General Ironsi declared Nigeria to be a unitary state. Participation, in other words, was to be undermined by the arbitrary erasure of the social distinctions that might give rise to interests and by the isolation of the masses from those who could manipulate those interests for their own ends—the politicians.

Where participation was allowed, it was kept within narrow bounds. The Pakistan Basic Democracies system, organized a year after General Ayub Khan's rise to power, allowed universal suffrage at only the lowest level of a five-tier arrangement of councils.[12] In Indonesia, the government attempted to alter electoral constituencies in order to increase the number of independent legislators.[13] In Ghana, it was suggested that only the literate be given the vote, and even the more temperate constitutional proposals of the regime appear to have been slanted heavily against the masses.[14] Always, the people were to be separated from the ensnarement of the politicians. As one proponent of the Pakistan regime argued:

> If the one-party system with all its undemocratic hazards is not to be adopted, then the presidential system alone holds the field. For, *while it does not bind the people hand and foot to highly organized political parties and they can enjoy their freedom from party loyalty and duty* [italics mine], they are nonetheless given the chance to exercise their franchise and elect the government of their liking. . . .[15]

More than a series of momentary restrictions on politicians and overt political activities, however, "antipolitics," as the term itself states, represents an assault on any form of political give-and-take. Military regimes have usually suspended economic bargaining by occupational groups and sharply curtailed associational groups such as trade unions. The attack on

111

politics, not surprisingly, has usually been accompanied by a rapid expansion of the administrative structure. Political roles have been transformed into administrative roles. Political consolidation, so it seems, has come to be viewed as the inevitable result of an effective reorganization of the administrative structure, rather than in terms of reciprocity relationships within the center and between the center and the periphery. James Heaphey's discussion of this antipolitical view in Egypt seems equally applicable to other military regimes as well.

> The vision [of development] seeks uniformity, not differences, not potential for indiv¹dual discretion. It would be a contradiction in values for the Egyptian elite to build politics into their vision, for theirs is an image of a smooth-running machine, geared to the logical, well-planned needs of rapid economic development. As for a political model incorporating the unpleasant and uncertain aspects of politics, that is simply an unworthy goal.[16]

The "political kingdom," to reverse a phrase associated with Kwame Nkrumah, is to be sought last, if ever.

Cohesion and Conflict in the Political Center

The initial governing structures organized by the military elites after seizing power have tended to be very fluid, reflecting their somewhat ambivalent legitimacy, their usually hasty creation, and the usually relatively new alliances between the military elites who participate in them. The most common governing structure has been some form of emergency, collegial, self-styled revolutionary council, composed of the major participants of the coup. The Revolutionary Command Council in Egypt, the National Liberation Council in Ghana, the National Reformation Council in Sierra Leone are but several examples of this type of structure. The locus of authority in most of these councils has tended to be blurred—few coups appear to have had *a* leader—and many of these structures have almost immediately become arenas of conflict between the various participants as disputes over dominance, over policy, and over the future role of the military in the regime manifest themselves. Conflicts between Qassim and Arif in Iraq, Nasser and Naguib in Egypt, between activists (who favored prolonged military rule) and conservatives (who did not) in Turkey are, again, characteristic.

Fluidity and instability have tended to characterize not only the junta itself but also the relationships between the junta and the other actors in the political center. The linkage between the military elites in the junta and the remainder of the military elites may be almost nonexistent, particularly if the perpetrators of the coup represent only a small minority of the military elites and, as has often been the case, are largely junior officers. In Turkey, for example, where the May 1960 coup was largely the result of a conspiratorial group of thirty-eight officers of diverse ranks, the rest of the military looked upon the junta with considerable suspicion. Although new senior military commanders were appointed after the coup, ostensibly to secure a better working relationship between the junta and the rest of the military, these generals appear to have been particularly concerned to keep politics out of the military. This concern intensified when factionalism within the junta began to generate outward to enlist other military officers. The high command supported the exiling of the activist faction and then screened all junta members from the military, forbidding them to rejoin the ranks.[17] In South Korea, where antagonism between junior and senior officers played a role in initiating a coup led by the former, relations between the two groups were particularly tense.

Even where those military elites assuming power have been senior officers and where the military as a whole has appeared to participate in the coup, cleavages have developed. As Dankwart Rustow has noted:

> the junta, because of the very success of its conspiracy, will have to surrender to other officers the command positions in and near the capital that launched it to power; for no

one can direct at one and the same time the ministry of economics and a tank battalion. . . . Having played their trump cards, the soldier-rulers will have to deal them to other players, and they may well find themselves challenged to further rounds at the same game.[18]

In Ghana, a young lieutenant and his squadron, discontent over slow promotions, nearly toppled the military regime in 1967. In Dahomey, a lack of consultation on the part of the senior officers who assumed power and the efforts of those officers to enlist civilian support were cited by junior officers as the justification for their successful *putsch* in December 1967, two years after the military regime had been organized.

The ruling military elites have usually relied heavily on the civil service in the period following their take-over—a phenomenon that is not surprising in view of the antipolitical views of most of the military elites. Few military leaders—even assuming a close relationship between the junta and the rest of the military—have had the personnel to attempt direct control over the administration. Several leaders have also expressed concern as to what such involvement might do to the military itself. As Ayub Khan, for example, declared:

> It was vital that the army be kept in the background because that was where it belonged in the normal life of the country. Had it too got directly involved in civil administration, the effect would have been a further demoralization and disintegration of the civil authority. It would have also made the withdrawal of the army from civilian life to their normal sphere of work more difficult. I did not have any doubt that the army would be destroyed if it got too mixed up in running the civil administration or too involved with the economic, social, and political affairs of the country.[19]

As a result, military leaders have tended to make themselves modern equivalents to the colonial-era governors and lieutenant governors, limiting themselves to designating temporary military supervisors for the various administrative agencies, which have remained largely in the hands of the civil

THE MILITARY IN POWER

servants.[20] In Ghana, for example, junta members initially retained their military and police commands and, as a result, were somewhat haphazard in asserting their control. Civil servants replaced their political counterparts as heads of ministries and regional commissioners, and a number of committees, almost wholly comprised of civil servants,[21] were organized to advise the junta on a wide variety of matters.

The initial alliances with the bureaucracy were not without their tensions. Military take-overs have usually been accompanied by announcements of plans to purge the bureaucracies because of their corruption and their association with the ousted regimes. In several states, purges actually occurred. In Pakistan, Ayub Khan established a screening committee to investigate the various services, and 526 civil servants—mostly at the middle levels of the bureaucracy—were either compelled to retire or removed outright.[22] The military rulers frequently decried the inefficiency of the civil services, and in Ghana and Nigeria, they went so far as to round up civil servants who did not report to work on time.

In several states the actual role played by the military in the administration of the government has been considerably larger. In states such as Burma and Indonesia, where the militaries had long been involved in a variety of administrative, political, and economic activities, this involvement increased. In Indonesia, for example, many civil servants active at the cabinet and departmental levels were, in fact, recruited from the armed forces after the military government assumed power.[23]

During this initial post-coup period, not all actions taken by the regime with regard to political elites have been hostile ones. Few politicians were actually incarcerated, and of those that were, few were held for any appreciable period of time. The various restrictions on political activity have usually been haphazardly enforced. In some cases, efforts have been made to integrate political elites with the regime through political committees, advisory committees, and the like. This appears to have been especially the case in those countries such as Ghana

115

where the coup was aimed at a particular set of political elites rather than at the political system as a whole.

The instability within the junta and the notable fluidity of power relationships within the political center in general during the period immediately following a coup ultimately pose a crisis for the military rulers. It becomes increasingly apparent that political forces cannot be done away with or even controlled by pronouncement. In those states where such forces are not explicitly and forcibly prohibited, they often demand greater participation in the regime or a return to civilian rule. Bureaucracies, freed from political supervision, are increasingly autonomous. The rest of the military poses a continuous threat—especially as discontent over the ruling military elites' efforts to accommodate civilians asserts itself and as factionalism, both within the junta and between participants and nonparticipants in the junta, becomes more overt. The successful Dahomey *putsch* of December 1967 is an example of disgruntlement with growing civilian influence; coup attempts in South Korea and Ghana exemplify factionalism within juntas.

In these circumstances, withdrawal becomes a possibility. The initial inability of the military elites to gain effective control of the system may persuade them to disengage altogether.[24] More frequently, however, the choice is not really available. The conditions that engendered the military's involvement in the first place tend to be persisting characteristics of the political process in underdeveloped states. The military rulers' efforts to withdraw, as a result, have generally not been successful in the long run.[25]

More commonly, the ruling military elites have made a concerted effort to restructure the political center—and the political system as a whole—in order to insure their dominance. In some ways, this search for primacy has resembled attempts at political consolidation within civilian regimes. Like their civilian counterparts, ruling military elites have relied heavily on their control of government resources and the manipulation of those resources to force centralization. Personal loyalties and patrimonial ties between ruling military elites and their appointees have frequently been the principal means through which consolidation and control of the political center have been sought.

This pattern is visible within the military almost as soon as a particular military leader has been able to establish his personal primacy over the junta itself. In Egypt, Nasser, following a purge of unsympathetic officers, relied (until 1967) on his close friend, Abdel Hakim Amir, as Commander-in-Chief and Defence Minister, to keep the military under control. In South Korea, the Park government implemented a series of compulsory early retirement laws to allow the mainstays of the 1961 coup, the second and eighth classes of the Officers Candidate School, to assume control.[26] Park's personal allies were positioned in strategic command positions and in the Army Counter-Intelligence Agency, created to maintain a strict surveillance of all high-ranking officers and their relationships with one another.[27] In Indonesia, the pattern has been more complex, principally because of the complex factional structure within the military, but basically similar. Suharto, besides purging leftist military commanders and simultaneously occupying the positions of President, Minister of Defence, and Commander of the Armed Forces (in order to insulate the military from elites who might directly compete with him), has utilized his extensive appointment power to place his faction members in strategic positions in the military hierarchy and to attract the support of other factions.[28] He has also transferred leaders of antagonistic factions to distant regions or other countries or to relatively unimportant positions.[29]

The search for primacy is also discernible in the changing relationships between the various military regimes and the political elites. In those states where political parties have continued to be legal, the military rulers have tried to influence the selection of party leaders more favorably disposed to the military government—a pattern particularly visible in Indonesia.[30] More commonly the ruling military elite has attempted to generate, in effect, a new political elite through the creation of a government-sponsored political party. The

117

military rulers, rather than utilizing such parties to organize reciprocity relationships between themselves and existing political elites, have generally by-passed those elites and have relied on "new" politicians who, in theory at least, would attract support for the regime by providing patronage and other government benefits to the population. Such parties—for example, the Democratic-Republican Party in South Korea, the (conventionist) Muslim League in Pakistan, and the Liberation Rally, the National Union, and the early Arab Socialist Union in Egypt —appear to represent the military's attempt to provide a means of generating popular support without the danger of that means' becoming too independent of the regime itself.[31]

Although available data is extremely fragmentary, it appears that several of the military regimes have attempted two principal means of political consolidation. First, they tried to "depoliticize" the political system by increasing the number of administrative roles while decreasing the number of political roles in the system. Second, in order to reduce the autonomy of the expanded bureaucracy, they sought to "personalize" control over that administrative structure.

The first tactic is evident both in the general expansion of the bureaucracy in numbers, agencies, and activities and in the transformation of political roles into administrative appointments. In Egypt, the number of government posts has grown from 381,615 in 1954-1955 to 1,255,000 in 1964-1969.[32] In South Korea, the number of bureaus within the economic ministries alone has swelled from twenty-one to thirty-four.[33] Politicians have been largely replaced by civil servants at all levels, and political positions have been either abolished or redefined as roles within a bureaucratic hierarchy. The Pakistan Basic Democracies System is an example of such a transformation. In its five-tier arrangement of councils, only the local boards (Union Councils) were elected through direct adult suffrage, and each successive level was made up both of "elected" members chosen from the council chairmen at the next lowest level and of an increasing proportion of "official" members —i.e., civil servants. The system represented an effort to create an almost completely depoliticized hierarchy of governmental organizations. Although the system was to establish a means of popular participation, Basic Democrats (those elected to the local councils) were denied any real political role. As one scholar has noted:

> it is the government, not any popular constituency, that . . . decides just which elected councilors do, in fact, have the opportunity to "represent" on the district, division, and, till June 1962, provincial level. It should be kept in mind that there are 8,355 Union Council chairmen from which to choose appointees for 76 District and Agency councils, 15 Divisional Councils and two provincial councils. . . . Thus it is highly unrealistic to assume that the power base of the "representative" member in the District or Division Council is his own constituency rather than the appointing authority—and it would be naive to assume that these "representatives" of the people do not realize this.[34]

The second tactic has meant that the ruling military elites have recruited outside of the regular civil service for administrators to man the expanded administrative structure, particularly at the senior levels. Such recruitment—of experts who have often had little actual administrative experience—has offered a means of control over the enlarged bureaucratic apparatus, since the individuals selected were either personally attached to the ruling military elite or—because they were outside of the regular civil service hierarchy—dependent upon the military rulers for their positions. Thus, in Ghana, the senior civil servants who initially assumed control of the government ministries after the military take-over gave way to depoliticized specialists. Half of the civilian commissioners appointed in 1967 were specialists in the work of the ministries they were appointed to head.[35] Only five of the twenty men who held office as commissioners were ex-civil servants.[36]

In Egypt, where a modern civil service was really organized only after the coup, the bureaucracy has come to be dominated by technocrats possessing few or no power bases of their own.[37] Throughout his rule, Nasser maintained a pattern of "personalized" control over the bureaucracy. Key ministries were initially placed under the control of members of the Revolutionary Command Council. As the technocratic class developed, Nasser attempted to maintain his control by continuously placing supporters in key positions at the various levels and by periodically reshuffling.

In Pakistan, Ayub Khan relied on both the military and civilians to break the traditional monopoly of the elite Civil Service of Pakistan (CSP) over senior administrative positions. After the declaration of martial law (October 7, 1958), 272 military officers were appointed either to administer civilian departments or agencies directly or to oversee the working of those civilian officers who kept their positions.[38] In 1959, the central government created the Economic Pool—a supra-administrative service that could draw members from all the civil services to man positions in the Ministries of Finance, Commerce, Economic Affairs, etc.[39] Forty percent of the members were to be recruited from outside the CSP. Even after the army was returned to the barracks and responsibility for civil administration was largely restored to the CSP, this pattern continued through the induction of young military officers into the CSP. According to one study, "Out of the fourteen army and navy officers who joined the Civil Service of Pakistan between 1960 and 1963, *eight had very close connections with the top echelon of the military hierarchy* [italics mine]."[40]

In Zaire, the role of "experts, acting in the shadow of the presidency and under its direct supervision," has massively increased under Joseph Mobutu.[41] By the end of 1967, depoliticized former university students and technicians dominated the cabinet.[42] Mobutu has also personalized his control over the administration by substantially increasing the number of administrative positions dependent on his personal appointment and by removing administrators from situations where they might develop personal power bases. Governors and their appointees, provincial commissioners and provincial secretaries, for example, were transferred from their home regions and made directly accountable to the president—a tactic extended down to the district level as well.[43]

The outcome of these various attempts at consolidation is obscure—again largely because of insufficient information. It appears, however, that these efforts have generally not been successful. In the first place, factionalism within the various juntas has continued to plague these regimes long after the initial, unsettled period of rule was thought to be ended. In Egypt, for example, the cohesion of the Free Officer group, which engineered the coup, atrophied considerably during the 1950's and 1960's.[44] In South Korea, personal rivalries have altered the junta membership radically. At least seven members of the junta, including the Army Chief of Staff at the time of the coup, have been involved in unsuccessful coups to displace the current leader, Park Chung-hee. Such coup attempts in South Korea as well as elsewhere are a testimonial to the difficulties military regimes have had in establishing complete control over the military. The increasing frequency of coups in Africa and Asia results not only from deteriorating relationships between civilian governments and the military, but also from the embroilment of military elites in factional conflicts and from the estrangement between military governments and the rest of the military.

Second, the military rulers' efforts either to generate a new political elite or to coopt old politicians into the regime by developing regime-sponsored political parties have been undermined by the continued distrust that the military rulers have for politics. Politicians—old or new—are generally isolated from the regime. Such distrust is vividly apparent in C. I. Eugene Kim's description of President Park's relationship with the Democratic-Republican Party (DRP) in South Korea:

> Never keen about parties and politics, President Park sees his government as one of technocrats and administrators. . . . He has openly expressed distrust of his own party. . . . He tends to separate party politics from policy-making and administration. When a conflict developed between

the party leaders and the cabinet members, President Park usually stood with his cabinet members, minimizing the role of the party. . . . To him, the DRP is a useful instrument for electoral success, but it is not fit for his vision of administrative polity. For decision-making, his chief advisors are found in his presidential secretariat and cabinet. His presidential secretariat in particular has become so integral in the exercise of his office that it is sometimes called the "small cabinet," and the emergence of a strong presidential secretariat staffed largely by non-party personnel has resulted in the party surrendering its decision-making responsibility to it.[45]

Finally, the tendency for those elites placed at the head of various administrative agencies to entrench themselves and to attempt to develop their agencies as personal patrimonies is more assertive than ever in military regimes. In part, this is a result of the fact that military rulers have generally proved to be even less adroit as leaders than were their predecessors. More than this, however, the depoliticization of the political system attempted by these leaders, with its concomitant growth in the number of administrative roles, seems to create a bureaucracy that simply exceeds the control of any leader, regardless of the number of personal followers placed throughout the administrative structure. Where the regular civil service was originally to be limited or circumvented, the expansion of administrative agencies—in the absence of other trained personnel—has, in the end, often provided the means whereby the regular civil service could reestablish its autonomy. Thus, in Pakistan where the Basic Democracies System represented an attempt to bureaucratize the political system, it also reestablished the power of the CSP in that system.

> The Basic Democracies Order of 1959 has given the civil servants working in the divisions and districts "controlling power" over the new local bodies. Under the system created by the Order, CSP [Civil Service of Pakistan] Commissioners preside over the Divisional Councils and CSP (or Provincial Civil Service) Deputy Commissioners

are the chairmen of the District Councils. . . . *The system of Basic Democracies stopped the erosion of the power of the CSP* [italics mine]; by being the undisputed leaders of the local communities the civil servants commanded authority not as the agents of a law and order administration but as the representatives of an avowed "welfare state." And with the launching of the massive Rural Works Programme in 1962, aimed at developing the rural areas by further activating the local councils, the CSP divisional and district administrators obtained a new lever of power: control over development funds.[46]

In summary, despite the bold rhetoric of the military rulers, their concern for centralizing authority, and their suspicion of cleavages within a society, the political center as organized by ruling military elites is potentially more decentralized than ever. The tug between the centralizing "kings" and the decentralizing subordinate authorities is likely to be more visible than ever. In Indonesia, for example:

As the economy deteriorated under Guided Democracy, all government bodies experienced financial difficulties. Official wages fell far below what was needed for survival and funds for maintenance and new equipment became increasingly limited. Like other bodies, the army had to cope with this problem. Local units were given considerable freedom to raise funds in their own ways (e.g. by smuggling, unofficial taxes, army-sponsored enterprises etc.), while those officers who were active in the state corporations seem to have had the responsibility of diverting funds directly to the army. In 1966 and afterwards [the period following the coup] these problems remained. Enterprises like *Pertamina* (the state oil corporation), *Berdikari* (a large trading corporation) and *Bulog* (in charge of the procurement and marketing of rice) were headed by generals directly responsible to Soeharto rather than to the minister of the department where their activities would have been placed according to administrative logic. It seemed that their function was to provide finance for the army. At the same time local army units continued to raise their own funds.

In these activities the generals to a large extent cooperated with Chinese businessmen (known as *tjukongs*) who had the business skills and the capital while the generals could provide access to, and a smooth ride through, the bureaucracy. Thus, at all levels, from Djakarta down to the regional towns, close ties have developed between the military and the Chinese trading community. This has strengthened the tendency for investment to go towards fields which promise quick and high returns rather than towards long-term projects of more permanent value for economic development.

While the army had little alternative but to seek its own funds when these were not forthcoming from the state budget, one unavoidable side-effect was to place many military officers in positions where they can make considerable profits for themselves. Their role has come to resemble that of the traditional tax-collector, who (provided the ruler gets his share) can keep whatever is left over. Naturally, the central army leadership was cautious about disciplining those who supplied much of its own funds.[47]

Cohesion and Conflict in the Periphery

In its efforts to expand its control over the larger political system, the military regime is confronted with essentially the same problem that confronted its civilian predecessors: expanding and consolidating state authority in a highly segmented national political system. The response of the military regime, however, has been in many ways unique. Forever distrustful of politics, ruling military elites—with few exceptions—appear to have eschewed the creation of direct linkages between them and the periphery altogether. What has emerged is a highly indirect system of linkages between center and periphery, in which bureaucracies have become the principal channels for decision-making and for the allocation of government benefits.

The forcible removal of central political elites from positions of authority severs the primary linkages between the central government and the political periphery, the linkages that those leaders had with their personal followings. These men do not, however, necessarily cease to be leaders. The

THE MILITARY IN POWER

extremely limited research available on this point, in fact, reveals some persistence in these ties. In Nondwin, one of the Burmese villages studied by Manning Nash, the local political leader appeared to have retained his identification and ties with U Nu after the latter's ouster by General Ne Win.[48] These linkages are no longer between elites in the political center (in the sense of occupying positions of authority) and the periphery but rather between elites that are either isolated from the center or, in many cases, hostile to it.

In the instances where the ruling military elites have tried to develop linkages with the periphery, they have—again with several exceptions—been largely unsuccessful, principally because of the equivocal, often contradictory manner in which they attempted to establish those linkages. The various military regimes' attempts to create their own political parties are the most glaring example of this. While such parties have been organized ostensibly to mobilize public support and, in some cases, to provide a basis of support for the regime other than the military, they have been undercut almost from the start, as noted earlier, by the unwillingness of the military elites to allow such parties any real role in the regime.

Government-sponsored parties tend to be not only isolated from decision-making in the regime—and thus of little utility as channels for access to the center by elites and groups in the periphery—but also limited in their functioning as political machines. It is true that government resources are expended to attract or, at times, even coerce support. For example, in Indonesia:

> In Galur subdistrict, the GOLKAR chairman was the local military commander, and in each of the seven villages of the subdistrict . . . an army veteran or paramilitary official was appointed GOLKAR vice-chairman. . . . The houses of prominent [opposition] party leaders were searched by the military for hidden weapons on the eve of the election, troops were brought in to guard the polling places, and rumors of arrests spread throughout the subdistrict. . . . The Galur voter needed a measure of courage to cast a nonGOLKAR vote.[49]

But after public support has been won or coerced, government parties do not seem to serve as a means of allocating government benefits to various individuals and groups in the periphery. While the Indonesian government, following its decision to develop GOLKAR as a political party, forced all government and village officials to join the party or lose their jobs, that requirement seems to have been less the consequence of a desire to build a strong party than of a concern to prevent those officials—many of whom were partisans of the opposition parties—from utilizing their position to assist those opposition parties. In Egypt, the various regime parties were used for careful management of participation and mobilization but for little else.[50] Government-sponsored parties, in other words, appear to be even more intermittent than their predecessors in civilian regimes, at least in terms of providing resources to the periphery.

Outside of these relatively ineffective parties, the ruling military elites have not, it appears, been able to establish linkages to the periphery. These leaders seem to place a high valuation on exhortatory, symbolic mobilization. Nasser's use of plebiscites and rallies to buttress his rule is well known, and other military rulers, such as Park Chung-hee, Ayub Khan, and Mobutu, have similarly emphasized their own paternal links to their people. With the exception of Nasser, however, few of these leaders seem to have engendered widespread popular support.

The primary links between center and periphery in the military-led political system appear to be focused elsewhere than on the junta itself. The bureaucratic expansion that generally follows a military take-over and the military's reliance on technocratic expertise, in effect, locate the principal channels of access to decision-making within bureaucracy. The reciprocity relationships (patron-client bonds, etc.) that link center and periphery tend to be defined, as a result, in terms of individuals well placed in the civil and military bureaucracies and their personal allies and clients, a pattern described by Moore in his study on Algeria and in his recent brief reflection on associational life in modern Egypt.[51] Bureaucracies, as the quotation concerning the effects of the Basic Democracies System in Pakistan illustrates, increasingly control resources and their dispersion.

Linkages between the military rulers themselves and the periphery, then, seem limited and, at best, indirect. Such indirect ties may not create instability, but it is likely that they will exacerbate the decentralizing tendencies already at work in the political center.

A final point should be noted. Although there is little data relating to communalism in military-dominated political systems, it appears that their lack of structures for political aggregation has often caused the expression of demands to become highly particularistic and, since modern voluntary associations are frequently either sharply curtailed or banned altogether, retraditionalized. In other words, ethnic and tribal structures have become the principal associational means for articulating demands, a pattern noted by Kraus in Ghana and at least suggested by Audrey Smock in her study of the Ibo unions in Nigeria.[52] Robert Pinkney's brief study of Ghana after the military coup of 1966 suggests another reason for the continuing importance of traditional structures. Because the regime lacks even a nominal mass base, the only political platform the military government and its appointees have in the rural areas is that provided by the traditional authorities.[53]

As is obvious from the repeated references to the limited information available concerning military regimes, conclusions about such regimes must necessarily be tentative. It would seem, however, that in their denial of politics, such regimes only exacerbate the fragmentation of the underdeveloped political system. Given the support of the armed forces, a military government may assure its own tenure. Such support, however, has usually been ephemeral. Even where that support is secure, tenure has not often produced real authority, and the particular way in which military regimes often pursue authority seems to initiate a process in which a kind of feudalization of the political system becomes probable. Political consolidation and the capability to rule are likely to be as elusive for the military leader as they were for his civilian counterpart.

NOTES

1. Joseph Mobutu, President of Zaire, speech, December 12, 1965. Quoted in J. C. Willame, *Patrimonialism and Political Change in the Congo* (Stanford: Stanford University Press, 1972), p. 132.

2. Claude Welch, Jr., "The African Military and Political Development," in Henry Bienen, ed., *The Military and Modernization* (Chicago: Aldine-Atherton, 1971), p. 213.

3. The "industrial-entity" characterization is from Lucian W. Pye, "Armies in the Process of Political Modernization," in John J. Johnson, ed., *The Role of the Military in Underdeveloped Countries* (Princeton: Princeton University Press, 1962), p. 76.

4. Dankwart A. Rustow, *A World of Nations: Problems of Political Modernization* (Washington, D.C.: The Brookings Institution, 1967), p. 187.

5. Ann Ruth Willner, "Perspectives on Military Elites as Rulers and Wielders of Power," *Journal of Comparative Administration*, II (1970), 262.

6. M. D. Feld, "Professionalism, Nationalism, and the Alienation of the Military," in Jacques van Doorn, ed., *Armed Forces and Society* (The Hague: Mouton and Co., 1966), p. 68.

7. Aristide Zolberg, "Military Intervention in the New States of Tropical Africa," in Henry Bienen, ed., *The Military Intervenes* (New York: Russell Sage Foundation, 1968), p. 87.

8. See, for example, James Heaphey, "The Organization of Egypt: Inadequacies of a Nonpolitical Model for Nation-Building," *World Politics*, XVIII, 2 (1966), 177-183.

9. Park Chung-hee, President of South Korea, quoted in John Kie-Chang Oh, *Korea: Democracy on Trial* (Ithaca: Cornell University Press, 1968), p. 134.

10. For details on the Elective Bodies (Disqualification) Order, see Government of Pakistan, *The Gazette of Pakistan* (Extraordinary), August 1959. On the South Korean law and its effects, see Oh, pp. 138-141.

11. M. J. Dent, "The Military and the Politicians," in S. K. Panter-Brick, ed., *Nigerian Politics and Military Rule: Prelude to Civil War* (London: Athelone Press, 1970), pp. 82-83.

12. On the Basic Democracies System, see Government of Pakistan, "The Basic Democracies Order, 1959," *The Gazette of Pakistan*, October 1959. The system is discussed in Karl Von Vorys, *Political Development in Pakistan* (Princeton: Princeton University Press, 1965), pp. 196-207.

13. Harold Crouch, "Military Politics Under Indonesia's New Order," *Pacific Affairs*, XLV, 2 (1972), 214-215.

14. See the *Report of the Constitutional Committee*, Accra, 1968.

15. Z. A. Suleri, Chief Editor of the *Pakistan Times*, quoted in Lawrence Ziring, *The Ayub Years* (Syracuse: Syracuse University Press, 1970), p. 11.

16. Heaphey, p. 187.

17. Nur Yalman, "Intervention and Extrication: The Officer Corps in the Turkish Crisis," in Bienen, pp. 134-135.

18. Rustow, p. 189.

19. Mohammed Ayub Khan, *Friends, Not Masters* (London: Oxford University Press, 1967), p. 77.

20. Edward Feit, "Military Coups and Political Development," *World Politics*, XX (1968), 188.

21. A few political elites were allowed into these committees. See *infra*.

22. Ziring, pp. 12-13.

23. Crouch, p. 213.

24. This argument differs considerably from that of Claude Welch, who views withdrawal as resulting either from the ascendance within the junta of a military faction which "respects civilian supremacy" or from the "civilianization" of a military regime—i.e., the resignation of the ruling military elites from the military. With the possible exception of Turkey immediately after the 1960 coup and of a few specific individual military elites elsewhere, there is little evidence that "respect for civilian supremacy" is widespread. If the military withdraws, it is more likely because it realizes that it cannot really achieve control. Welch's second alternative mistakes a change in clothes for a change in regime. These "civilianized" regimes retain the distinguishing characteristic of the military regime, a continuing reliance on the military to stay in power. "Civilianization," linked as it is to building mechanisms for dominating the political center and periphery, represents not an attempt to withdraw so much as it does an attempt to dominate.

25. It has become almost customary to distinguish between coups of a temporary nature in which the military acts as a mediator ("referee coups") and coups with most permanent consequences (take-overs). In reality, however, it may be difficult to distinguish between the two. Military elites may intervene with intentions to alter the political system completely but withdraw because of their inability to do so. Such a coup may serve as a referee coup for observers, but that was certainly not the coup's original intention. In sum, the motivations of the intervening military elites are critical in distinguishing one type of coup from another, and such motivations are usually difficult to ascertain.

26. Se-Jin Kim, *The Politics of the Military Revolution in Korea* (Chapel Hill: University of North Carolina Press, 1971), p. 155.

27. *Ibid.*, p. 156.

28. See Ulf Sundhaussen, "The Fashioning of Unity in the

Indonesian Army," *Asia Quarterly* (Brussels, 1971-1972); and Ann Gregory, "Factionalism in the Indonesia Army," *Journal of Comparative Administration*, II, 3 (November 1970), 341-354. For data on command changes in the Indonesia Army, see *Indonesia* (Cornell Modern Indonesia Project), I (April 1967), 205-216; IV (October 1967), 227-229; VII (April 1969), 195-201; X (October 1970), 195-208.

29. Gregory, pp. 349-350.

30. On one such effort, see Allan A. Samson, "Army and Islam in Indonesia," *Pacific Affairs*, XLIV, 4 (1971-1972), 545-565.

31. On the Muslim League, see Von Vorys, pp. 255-259. On the DRP, see C. I. Eugene Kim, "Institution-Building and Adaptation: The Case of the DRP in South Korea," paper delivered at the 1972 annual meeting of the American Political Science Association, Washington, D.C. On the Egyptian parties, see Leonard Binder, "Political Recruitment and Participation in Egypt," in Joseph La Palombara and Myron Weiner, eds., *Political Parties and Political Development* (Princeton: Princeton University Press, 1966), pp. 217-240.

32. Iliya F. Harik, "Mobilization Policy and Political Change in Rural Egypt," in Richard Antoun and Iliya Harik, eds., *Rural Politics and Social Change in the Middle East* (Bloomington: Indiana University Press, 1972), p. 293.

33. In-Joung Whang, "Leadership and Organizational Development in the Economic Ministries of the Korean Government," *Asian Survey*, XI, 10 (1971), 992-1004.

34. Von Vorys, pp. 203-204.

35. Robert Pinkney, *Ghana Under Military Rule, 1966-1969* (London: Methuen and Co., Ltd., 1972), p. 77. Fourteen civilian commissioners were appointed in June 1967. Together with the remaining members of the National Liberation Council, they served on a new National Executive Committee charged with general control of the government of Ghana.

36. *Ibid.*

37. On the Egyptian bureaucracy, see Morroe Berger, *Bureaucracy and Society in Modern Egypt* (Princeton: Princeton University Press, 1957).

38. Shahid Javed Burki, "Twenty Years of the Civil Service of Pakistan: A Reevaluation," *Asian Survey*, IX, 4 (1969), 247.

39. *Ibid.*, p. 248.

40. *Ibid.*

41. Jean-Claude Willame, "Congo-Kinshasa: General Mobutu and Two Political Generations," in Welch, pp. 144-145.

42. *Ibid.*

43. J. C. Willame, *Patrimonialism and Political Change in the Congo* (Stanford: Stanford University Press, 1972), pp. 135-136.

44. See R. Hrair Dekmejian, *Egypt Under Nasir* (Albany, N.Y.: State University of New York Press, 1971).

45. Se-Jin Kim, pp. 9-10.

46. Burki, p. 250.

47. Crouch, p. 217.

48. Manning Nash, *The Golden Road to Modernity* (New York: John Wiley and Sons, 1965), pp. 87-89.

49. R. William Liddle, "The 1971 Indonesian Elections: A View from the Village," *Asia*, No. 27 (1972), 14.

50. Leonard Binder, *Iran: Political Development in a Changing Society* (Berkeley and Los Angeles: University of California Press, 1964), pp. 218-221, 229-233, 238-240.

51. Clement H. Moore, *Politics in North Africa* (Boston: Little, Brown and Company, 1970); and also his "Authoritarian Politics in Unincorporated Society: The Case of Nasser's Egypt," paper delivered at the 1972 annual meeting of the American Political Science Association, Washington, D.C.

52. Kraus, p. 204; and Audrey C. Smock, *Ibo Politics* (Cambridge, Mass.: Harvard University Press, 1971), p. x.

53. Pinkney, p. 27.

Conclusion

Underdevelopment is shocking: the squalor, the disease, unnecessary deaths, and the hopelessness of it all! . . . the prevalent emotion of underdevelopment is a sense of personal and societal impotence in face of disease and death, of confusion and ignorance as one gropes to understand changes, of servility toward men whose decisions govern the course of events, of hopelessness before hunger and natural catastrophe. Chronic poverty is a cruel kind of hell . . . .[1]

—Denis Goulet

The problem of political consolidation, of aggregating sufficient power to rule, has been an age-old concern in the study of politics. Despite this, it has proven to be a surprisingly difficult problem for contemporary students of comparative politics to focus on. In part, this may be attributable to, as W. Howard Wriggins has characterized it, a tendency on the part of modern scholars "to set aside the sweaty, contentious matter of political competition as . . . models become more abstract and sophisticated."[2]

More than this, however, the cause of the recent indifference, if it can be called that, to such "sweaty, contentious" matters may lie in the current perception of the underdeveloped state itself. Political scientists, principally concerned with clarifying the process of political development, have tended to confuse what one scholar has called "predevelopment" with "development"—i.e., the problem of creating a political system as opposed to the problem of adapting that system to the complexities of the modern world.[3] Although some effort has been made to distinguish between these two problems (e.g., Almond and Powell's concept of nation-building as opposed to state-building[4]), the fact that the two problems have generally been thrust upon the states of Africa and Asia simultaneously has caused them to be viewed as being so intertwined as to be inseparable.

The telescoping of the politics of predevelopment or underdevelopment into the politics of development has, in turn, caused scholars to see the principal problem confronted by the underdeveloped state as being the legitimation of a particular set of political institutions organized to govern that state.[5] Where the political institutions were essentially imports into these societies, the concern has been to understand the process by which those foreign institutions were reformulated and given legitimacy in their new environments. The means by which such institutions might be legitimated—tradition, charisma, legal-rationalism, ideology—remain the principal focus of analysis. Implicit in this formulation is the argument that legitimacy is effectiveness or, to reverse the classic phrase, that right makes might.[6]

> In speaking of the vital importance of leadership in raising the level of performance, we are alluding to the critical place of authority in national development. If leaders are to inspire a population and to direct a society to higher levels of performance, their words and actions must carry an aura of legitimacy. If a people are to gain satisfaction from the ways in which the polity performs, they must first accept it right and proper that the inherent functions of the political system can and must be performed in new ways. In short, if a polity is to resolve its identity crisis through more effective governmental performance and a rise in political capabilities, it must also resolve any issues of legitimacy.[7]

CONCLUSION

Recent history has shown such analysis to be premature. In many states, as the recurrent instability in these states attests, no single leadership group has successfully consolidated even the beginnings of control over the national political system—let alone established its legitimacy to rule. Even where new institutions of government appear to have achieved some degree of legitimacy and acceptability, their effectiveness has been extremely limited—regardless of the personal magnetism of the leaders or the various strategies they pursued.[8] A persistent segmentation of the political process continues to make political consolidation an elusive goal in these states.

It is not being suggested here that the study of the underdeveloped states be returned to an earlier era which saw national disintegration at hand everywhere in these states.[9] The opposite, in fact, seems to be true. Even if most of these states have not succeeded in achieving societal integration and in resolving the "crisis of identity" to the degree scholars have argued necessary, it must be recognized that—with notable exceptions, of course—the existence of these nation-state entities is no longer really at issue. But it must also be recognized that while the central conflicts in these societies concern confrontations between national elites over who will control the state apparatus and determine its goals, no one group of national elites appears to be able to aggregate sufficient power to utilize its control over the state apparatus effectively.

All of this does, of course, raise the question of legitimacy. Regardless of the historical, ideological, and charismatic sources of legitimacy that may exist for a system of political institutions, those institutions must ultimately be judged on their capacity to satisfy the aspirations of the people of the society. At the heart of the crisis of legitimacy in the underdeveloped states is a crisis of political consolidation. The power to rule effectively remains elusive.

In the way of social scientists, what was initially perceived as a problem has come to be viewed as a boon. In the mid-1960's, as information about these political systems became

135

more extensive, the earlier models of these systems—mobilizational versus reconciliation regimes, radical versus conservative regimes, and so forth—were jettisoned for models that made room for the fact that power in even the most monolithic and ideological regime remained elusive. An example of the newer models is the political-machine concept. While the development of the machine model marked a kind of confrontation with a disappointing reality for many scholars who had been hopeful of rapid strides toward democracy and modernity by underdeveloped countries, its application ultimately engendered a new—albeit more guarded—optimism. Some political scientists, although ambivalent about the potentiality of machine systems to restructure their societies, argued that these political systems were capable of achieving at least some modicum of stability and political development. Rajni Kothari, Myron Weiner, and James C. Scott have stressed the open character of such systems, their receptivity to local pressures.[10] Weiner, in his discussion of the Congress Party of India, has suggested that, because of this receptivity, the Congress-dominated political system is especially able to "cushion the tensions created by the modernization process."[11] Henry Bienen has argued that the decentralization so characteristic of machine systems could facilitate the emergence of effective local political institutions.[12] In Zolberg's view:

> Such a regime is not streamlined; it lacks a sense of glory and does not insure that there will be an immediate and revolutionary change in the human condition. But it is known to have operated successfully in West Africa. It is not genuinely democratic, but it tends to avoid senseless cruelty. Beyond this, it might help relieve the heavy burdens of imitation and self-doubt with which Africans have been saddled too long and might enable them to regain confidence in their ability to rule themselves. . . .[13]

Our brief study of politics in the underdeveloped states suggests that the tidiness and coherence of the machine model and the guarded optimism generated in terms of that model are overstated. The achievement of some sort of coherence in the political center—let alone the consolidation of power there—has proved to be extremely difficult. The segmentary character of the political center has tended to persist. The leaders of the various states have had to create and manage coalitions of factions in which—because of limited centralizing resources—the reciprocity relationships have been highly vulnerable to breakdown. At the same time, the complexity of the center and the strain on the leaders' limited centralizing resources have expanded with the extensive increase in the scope of government functions and operations. Such an increase expands both the number of authority roles in the center and the potential for what we have called patrimony-building. The system is not to be likened to a machine so much as to a multitude of machines frequently competing against one another. Power has, in effect, become more fragmented, and political consolidation more elusive.

The question must ultimately be asked as to how "uncruel" this kind of a political system really is. True, its capacity to coerce is minimal. Yet, so too is its capacity to satisfy the aspirations of its citizens. The inability of any single group of elites to consolidate their control over the political system is likely to produce immobilism. Because of the extreme fragmentation of power, ruling coalitions organized out of a widely diverse set of elites and groups are likely to be equally immobilized.[14] Even where the center is characterized by a considerable degree of cohesion, the instable, intermittent character of linkages between center and periphery appears to limit the center's capacity to deal with problems in the periphery. This becomes of particular concern as the dualistic nature of the economies of underdeveloped states—an expanding modern sector and a stagnant, often deteriorating traditional sector— widens, defeating overall economic expansion and raising the possibility of serious economic and political challenges to the political system.[15] Nor have local governmental institutions developed as adequate substitutes. Efforts by centralizing elites to maximize control over the periphery through agents of the central

137

administration have not usually succeeded in that goal and have instead tended to cause local institutions to atrophy.[16] In effect, the fragmented, intermittent political process which is characteristic of the underdeveloped state perpetuates itself. The power to accomplish national goals remains a scarce resource. In its absence, a government not only cannot deal with bettering the human condition of its people, it cannot even save itself.

NOTES

1. Denis Goulet, *The Cruel Choice: A New Concept in the Theory of Development* (New York: Atheneum, 1973), p. 23.

2. W. Howard Wriggins, *The Ruler's Imperative* (New York: Columbia University Press, 1969), p. 4.

3. Joungwon Alexander Kim, "The Politics of Predevelopment," *Comparative Politics*, V, 2 (1973), 213.

4. Gabriel Almond and G. B. Powell, *Comparative Politics: A Developmental Approach* (Boston: Little, Brown and Company, 1966), pp. 35-36.

5. Samuel Huntington, *Political Order in Changing States* (New Haven: Yale University Press, 1968) is the best example of this view.

6. This is especially visible in Dankwart A. Rustow, *A World of Nations: Problems of Political Modernization* (Washington, D.C.: The Brookings Institution, 1967), p. 157, where he suggests the following equations:

Political Stability   =   Legitimacy of Institutions
+   Personal Legitimacy of Rulers

Political Legitimacy =   Traditional Legitimacy
+   Rational-Legal Legitimacy
+   Charismatic Legitimacy

7. Lucian W. Pye, "Identity and Political Culture," in Leonard Binder, *et al.*, *Crises and Sequences in Political Development* (Princeton: Princeton University Press, 1971), p. 134.

8. For a discussion of the strategies of political consolidation, see Wriggins.

9. See, for example, Selig Harrison, *India: The Dangerous Decades* (Princeton: Princeton University Press, 1957).

10. Rajni Kothari, *Politics in India* (Boston: Little, Brown and Company, 1970); Myron Weiner, *Party Building in a New Nation* (Chicago: University of Chicago Press, 1967); and James C. Scott, *Com-*

parative Political Corruption (Englewood Cliffs, N.J.: Prentice-Hall, 1972).

11. Weiner, p. 16.

12. Henry Bienen, "What Does Political Development Mean in Africa?" *World Politics*, XX 1 (1967), 140.

13. Aristide Zolberg, *Creating Political Order: The Party-States of West Africa* (Chicago: Rand, McNally and Co., 1966), p. 160.

14. On the problems engendered by a politics of accommodation, see R. Cranford Pratt, "The Administration of Economic Planning in a Newly Independent State: The Tanzanian Experience, 1963-1966," *The Journal of Commonwealth Political Studies*, V, 1 (1967), 38-59. See also Jonathan S. Barker, "The Paradox of Development: Reflections on a Study of Local-Central Political Relations in Senegal," in Michael Lofchie, ed., *The State of Nations: Constraints on Development in Independent Africa* (Berkeley and Los Angeles: University of California Press, 1971), pp. 47-63.

15. For a consideration of this issue in the Ivory Coast, see Richard E. Stryker, "A Local Perspective on Development Strategy in the Ivory Coast," in Lofchie, pp. 119-139.

16. This is visible in the Ivory Coast; see *ibid.*, pp. 138-139.

Index

Accommodation, politics of, 139
Adamafio, T., 82
Adaptability, and tradition, 3
Adaptation of political parties, 60-61
AFPFL. *See* Anti-Fascist People's
Freedom League
Africa, associational activities in, 42;
clans in, 6; cooperatives in, 30;
emergence of nationalism in, 15, 18,
41; middle-class associations in, 24,
25; religious movements in, 29-30;
traditional societies in, 32; *see also*
West Africa
Agriculture, changes in, 27, 28
Ahardane, 88
Ahmad, A., 43
Ahomadegbe, 97
Algeria, linkage politics in, 38, 45;
military elites in, 96, 125;
patrimonialism in, 56
All-Ceylon Muslim League, 52
Allocation of resources. *See* Resource
allocations
Almond, G., 12, 134, 138
American political machines, 60, 73
Anderson, C. W., 103, 104
Andrain, C. F., 45, 72
Anti-Fascist People's Freedom League
(AFPFL), 62, 73
Antipolitics, in military regimes,
109-112
Antouin, R., 130
Apter, D. E., 12, 42, 44, 48, 70, 71, 100
Argov, D., 44
Arya Samaj, 30, 43
Ashford, D., 74
Asia, emergence of nationalism in, 15,
18; traditional societies in, 32; *see
also* Southeast Asia
Aspirations, of citizens, 135, 137; of
elites, 8, 39-40, 48, 49; of
government employees, 76; of youth
groups, 76-77
Associations, voluntary, integrated into
government, 55, 56-57, 69, 81, 82; in
military regimes, 111, 127;
prohibition of, 110
Austin, D., 42
Authority, conflicts over, 67; extended
by elites, 10; in military regimes,
112-113
Ayub Khan, M., 96, 97, 105, 111, 114,
115, 120, 126, 129

Bailey, F. G., 13
Balandier, G., 42
Bandaranaike, S. W. R. D., 84
Banfield, E., 73
Banks, role of, 82, 100
Banton, M., 43
Barker, J. S., 139
Basic Democracies System, in
Pakistan, 111, 118-119, 122-123,
127, 128
Bellows, T. J., 100
Ben Bella, 56
Bendix, R., 56, 72
Berger, A., 87, 101
Berger, M., 130
Bienen, H., 13, 48, 67, 71, 73, 74, 100,
104, 105, 128, 136, 139
Binder, L., 13, 45, 72, 130, 131
Bloc Démocratique Sénégalais, 35-36
Bomani, P., 37, 60

141

Boundary problems, and center-periphery relations, 58, 72
Bourguiba, 54
Brass, P., 44, 101
Bretton, H. L., 72, 100
Buganga, 32
Bureaucratic elites, 51; alliances with military regime, 114-115, 116, 118-120, 126; machines organized by, 63
Burki, S. J., 130
Burma, 44, 73; communalism in, 92; governmental services in, 64; military elites in, 96, 115; patron-client links in, 62; peasant protests in, 28, 29
Burundi, 54, 73, 93
Butwell, R., 73

Cady, J., 44
Callaway, B., 100
Campbell, M. J., 73
Capitalism, impact of, 27
Card, E., 100
Cartwright, J. R., 71, 100
Caste associations, 6, 25, 42, 90
Caste system, 89, 102
Censuses, effects of, 90, 102
Center and periphery, concepts of, 13; conflict sources in, 66-70; lack of cohesion in, 47, 49; sources of cohesion in, 59-66
Central African Republic, 98
Central government, access to and control of, 50; deconcentration of, 64-65, 67; elites in, *see* Political elites; emergence of, 50; expansion of, 82-83, 84; in military regimes, 112-124; organizing of, 52-57; personal connections to, 68; role of associations in, 55, 56-57, 69, 81, 82; and *sous-section* groups, 86; strengthening of power in, 64, 73, 79; support for, 60, 66
Ceylon, 71; alliances in, 52; communalism in, 101; decentralization in, 80; factionalism in, 84; linkage politics in, 60; opposition parties in, 87
Change. *See* Social change
Charisma, and center-periphery cohesion, 59; and patrimonialism, 71; and political consolidation, 48, 54

Check lists, of particularisms, 7; of social cleavages, 89, 102
Chinese trading community, ties with military, 124
Civil service, and military regimes, 114, 115
Civil Service of Pakistan (CSP), 120, 122-123, 130
Civilianization, of military regimes, 129
Clans, in Africa, 6, 36
Class interests, and middle-class associations, 23-26
Cleavages, check lists of, 89, 102; effects of, 89, 100; in military regimes, 109, 113; mutually reinforcing, 92; and opposition, 87; and patron-client bonds, 93; and political divisions, 80
Coalitions of elites, 8, 9, 10, 50-51, 52-57, 70; and access to government, 87; complexity of, 81; and factionalism, 85; fragmentation of, 57; tenuous nature of, 78, 79, 84-85, 88, 92, 93, 98
Cocoa Purchasing Co., Ltd., 82, 100
Coercion, and elite cohesion, 55; military role in, 97-98, 125-126
Cohen, D. L., 74, 100
Cohesion, center-periphery, 59-66
Coleman, J. S., 12, 18, 41, 42
Colonialism, 42; and cooperative development, 30-31; inheritors of, 81; and patron-client relationships, 27; political structures in, 50, 52; and protest movements, 23; and religious movements, 30; and role of money lenders, 28
Communalism, 77, 79, 88-94, 99, 101, 102; in military regimes, 127
Communication channels, 17, 110; growth in India, 34; and personal relationships, 61; in religious movements, 30
Competition, for control of government, 50, 52-53, 56, 81, 82; in military regimes, 113
Conflicts, center-periphery, 66-70; intra-elite, 9, 58, 68-69, 78, 79-88, 91; in military regimes, 112-128; military role in, 98; in segmentary societies, 100; variables in, 75
Congo, 42, 71, 102, 130; elite linkage process in, 36-37; middle-class

and communalism, 91; in military regimes, 113, 116, 117, 121, 130; military role in, 97, 98
Fallers, L., 72, 100
Farming, changes in, 27, 28
Feit, E., 129
Feld, M. D., 104, 128
Fernandez, J. W., 43
Finances. *See* Economics
Finer, S., 104
Fortes, M., 13
Foster, G. M., 43
Foster, P., 72, 73, 105
Fragmentation, of elites, 8, 9, 49, 57, 137; of institutions, 11; of military, 98; and social change, 6

Gabon, 43
Gambia, cooperatives in, 31, 43
Gandhi, M. K., 34, 38
Gaps, between center and periphery, 59; between generations, 76-77; between underdeveloped and modern states, 4
Geertz, C., 13, 42, 45, 72, 101, 102
Gellner, E., 101
Ghana, 12, 42, 44, 48, 72, 74, 100, 104, 105; coercion in, 55; conflicts in, 66; decentralization in, 81-82; factionalism in, 85-86; military regime in, 96, 111, 112, 114, 115, 116, 119, 127, 130; nationalism in, 20, 35; opposition parties in, 87; patrimonialism in, 54; patron-client relationships in, 32; political machinery in, 64, 68; strikes in, 26
Gluckman, M., 103
GOLKAR, in Indonesia, 125-126
Gosnell, H. F., 73
Goulet, D., 133, 138
Government. *See* Central government
Gregory, A., 130
Grew, R., 72
Group consciousness, and political mobilization, 7
Group interaction, managed by institutions, 4
Guinea, nationalist movement in, 38
Gupta, J. D., 102

Haidara family, in Timbuktu, 38
Hakim Amir, A., 117
Halmos, P., 104

Halpern, M., 12
Harik, I. F., 130
Harrison, S., 138
Hassan II, 53, 62
Hauser, W., 43
Hayes, C., 41
Heaphey, J., 72, 112, 128, 129
Heeger, G. A., 13, 45, 72, 101, 102, 103
Heimsath, C., 44
Hodgkin, T., 42, 43
Hopkins, K., 104
Houphouet-Boigny, 48, 54, 55, 62, 63
Huntington, S., 5, 12, 13, 44, 70, 73, 74, 99, 103, 104, 138
Hýden, G., 45

Ibo politics, 127, 131
Identity, changes in, 89-90; communal, 93; and middle-class associations, 24; and modernization, 19; and particularism, 6, 13; situations affecting, 62, 103
Ideology, and center-periphery cohesion, 59; and elite cohesion, 55; and factionalism, 83, 85-86; and intra-elite conflict, 80; and military regimes, 107; and nationalist movements, 20; one-party, 55, 72, 74; and opposition, 87; and patronage, 61; in peasant rebellions, 28-29; and political consolidation, 48; rigidity in, 82
Immobilism, causes of, 9, 137
Independence, affecting politics, 50; as aspiration of elites, 39; and crisis of management, 47; and lack of nationalism, 21; and lack of unity, 41; nationalist movement after, 59
India, 71, 74; castes in, 6, 42, 89, 90, 102; census role in, 90, 102; communalism in, 91; cultivator associations in, 29; factionalism in, 85, 86, 101; linguistic divisions in, 34; middle-class associations in, 24, 25; opposition parties in, 87; organizational development in, 33-34; peasant protests in, 28, 29; radical nationalism in, 20; religious movements in, 30; strikes in, 26
Indian Association, in Calcutta, 24
Indian National Congress, 20, 24, 33, 34, 35, 42, 60-61, 63, 65, 136; conflicts in, 69, 83, 85, 101

Indonesia, military regime in, 96, 97, 111, 115, 117, 125, 126, 129, 130
Inevitability, of development and modernization, 3, 10-11
Insecurity, nationalism as response to, 42, 45
Instability, and coercive capacity, 98; and communalism, 88-94; and factionalism, 79-88; as inherent characteristic, 78; in military regimes, 113, 116; sources of, 11, 75-79
Institutions, coalitions in, 50, 51; and elite status, 36; fragmentation of, 11; and governmental authority, 10; intertwinement of, 51; lack of capability in, 9, 75, 77; legitimation of, 134-135, 138; and management of group interaction, 4; organizational poverty of, 51; penetration into social mass, 59; personalism affecting, 70; segmentary nature of, 8, 13; support for, 47, 50, 52
Integration, national, 89, 101, 102, 103; politics of, 13, 92
Interactions in groups, managed by institutions, 4
Interest groups, role of, 56-57, 90-91
Iran, 13, 73, 131
Iraq, military regime in, 113
Ironsi, General, 111
Istiqlal government, 88
Ivory Coast, 44, 73, 101, 139; factionalism in, 86; local bureaucrats in, 67; organization development in, 34-35; party machines in, 62; patrimonialism in, 54, 55; patron-client relationships in, 32

Jacoby, E. H., 43
Janowitz, M., 104
Johnson, J. J., 104, 128
Jones, K., 43
Junta, linkage to military elites, 113, 115, 116, 117

Kasfir, N., 102
Kautsky, J., 80, 100
Kearney, R. N., 101
Kenya, 43, 85, 86, 101
Kie-Chang Oh, J., 128
Kilson, M., 41, 42, 45, 58, 69, 71, 72, 74, 103

Kim, C. I. E., 121, 130
Kim, J. A., 138
Kim, S-J., 129, 130
Kisan sabhas, 29
Kling, M., 104
Kohn, H., 41
Korea, military regime in, 98, 110, 113, 116, 117, 118, 120, 121-122, 128, 129, 130
Kothari, R., 71, 86, 101, 136, 138
Kraus, J., 105, 127, 131
Kripalani, A., 85
Krishna, G., 42, 44
Kwame Nkrumah Ideological Institute, 82

Labor. *See* Union activities
Landé, C. H., 63, 73
Landlords, attitudes toward, 28, 29
Language divisions, in India, 34
Laos, communalism in, 92
La Palombara, J., 130
Lasswell, H., 105
Leaders, capability of, 78, 82-83, 107
Legitimacy of institutions, 134-135, 138
Lemarchand, R., 32, 44, 73, 93, 103, 105
Lerner, D., 18, 41, 105
LeVine, V. T., 100
Levy, M. J., 104
Lewis, I. M., 105
Lewis, W. H., 101
Leys, C., 101
Liddle, R. W., 44, 131
Lijphart, A., 92, 103
Linguistic divisions, in India, 34
Linkages, complexity of, 64, 66, 69; and cooperative societies, 31; expansion of, 84; and factionalism, 85; instability of, 98; introduction to new sets of, 69; of military elites to junta, 113, 115, 116, 117; of military regime to periphery, 124-127; and nationalist movements, 33-39; and patrimonialism, 54; and patron-client relationships, 33; personal relationships in, 60-64; and political development, 49, 59; reciprocity relationships in, 60-61; in traditional societies, 32
Lipset, S. M., 102
Lissak, M., 104, 105
Local groups, linkage to nationalist

parties, 37-39; persistence of, 6; related to central system, 57-58; weakened powers of, 64; *see also* Periphery

Lofchie, M., 73, 100, 139

Loyalties, personal. *See* Personal relationships

Luckham, R., 105

Lumumba, P., 36-37, 44

Machine politics, 49, 60-64, 73; American, 60, 73; bureaucratic, 63; bypassing of, 68; personal, 61-62, 83-84; political, 62

Maguire, G. A., 31, 37, 42, 43, 44

Malaysia, communalism in, 92

Mali, 38, 45

Margai, A., 83, 87

Margai, M., 83

Marriott, McK., 72

Mass-oriented parties, 34-35, 44

Material rewards, and patronage, 61-62

Mauretania, 32

Mazrui, A. A., 43

Mboya, T., 85

Melson, R., 99, 102, 103

Messianic cults, 22, 23, 27, 29-30

Middle-class elites, associations organized by, 23-26; and cooperative development, 31; emergence of, 6; in Indian National Congress, 33; and nationalism, 20

Military elites, 51, 103-105; aspirations of, 76; and *coups d'état*, 94-99; linkage to junta, 113, 115, 116, 117; in political process, 96-98, 109; support of, 108-109

Military regimes, 71, 107-128; alliances with bureaucracy, 114-115, 116, 118-120, 126; and antagonism between junior and senior officers, 113-114; antipolitics of, 109-112, 113, 114, 121-122; and civil service, 114, 115; civilianization of, 129; coercion by, 125-126; consolidation attempts in, 116-121; councils in, 112, 118; financial difficulties of, 123-124; and government-sponsored parties, 125-126; in initial post-coup period, 112-116; and modernization goals, 108; personal allies in, 116-117; political center of, 112-124; and politics of order, 1; purges by,

115, 117; recruitment of experts in, 119-120, 130; relationship to political elites, 115-116, 117-118, 129; search for primacy in, 116-118; support for, 118, 125, 126; withdrawal of, 116, 129

Millennialism, and peasant movements, 28, 29

Mirza, I., 96, 97

Mitchell, C., 103

Mitchell, R. C., 43

Mobilization, and communalism, 91, 102; and group consciousness, 7; and parochialism, 110

Mobutu, J., 107, 111, 120, 126, 128, 130

Modernization, 12, 75-77, 100; and communication, 17; conflict with tradition, 66; definition of, 3, 12; inevitability of, 3, 10-11; and military role, 94-95, 108; and nationalism, 15, 18, 21-23; and nationalist movements, 19-20, 21; and particularism, 7; separation from development, 12-13; and social change, 3, 22

Modernizing elites, 7-8, 9, 11

Money lenders, attitudes toward, 28, 29

Moore, C. H., 72, 126, 131

Moors' Association, in Ceylon, 52

Moplah rebellion, in India, 28, 29

Morocco, 24, 53, 54, 62, 88, 101

Muslim League, 52, 54, 118, 130

Mwanza African Traders Cooperative Society, 37

Narain, I., 101

Nash, M., 64, 74, 125, 131

Nasser, 117, 119-120, 126, 130, 131

Nasution, General, 97

National Association of Socialist Students Organizations, 82, 85

National Council of Ghana Women, 82

National Liberation Movement, in Ghana, 66, 87

National Reformation Council, in Sierra Leone, 112

Nationalism, 15-45; compared to nationalist movements, 39-40; concepts of, 15-23, 39-40; economics as basis of, 45; lack of, after independence, 21; military sense of,

98; and modernization, 15, 18, 21-23; paradox in, 40; and parochialism, 58; psychological and emotional factors in, 15-16, 17, 20, 21; radical, surges of, 20; as response to insecurity, 42-45; and social change, 16-17; and subnationalism, 58, 66, 72; and traditional institutions, 22

Nationalist movements, compared to nationalism, 39-40; independence affecting, 59; legitimate allies in, 39, 40; and linkage politics, 33-39; mass-oriented parties in, 35; and modernization, 19-20, 21; and protest movements, 23-31; and rural politics, 26-31; segmentation of, 35-36, 50; sources of, 23-33; stages in, 22; support for, 35-36; and traditional societies, 32-33; and urban politics, 23-26; varying character of, 38-39

Nation-building, deterrents to, 58

Nativistic cults, 27

Needler, M., 103

Nehru, 48

Nepal, patrimonialism in, 54

Networks, coalitional, organization of, 51; of personal supporters, 54, 56, 94, 103; in religious movements, 30

Nigeria, 43, 44, 103, 105; decentralization in, 80-81; Ibo politics in, 127, 131; military regime in, 110-111, 128; party machine in, 61, 62; patron-client relationships in, 32

Nisbet, R., 12, 20, 42

Nkrumah, K., 44, 48, 54, 55, 68, 72, 82-83, 96, 100, 104, 110, 112

Nkrumah Ideological Institute, 82

NLM. See National Liberation Movement

North, R. C., 97, 105

Northern People's Congress, in Nigeria, 61, 62, 80-81

Northern People's Party, in Ghana, 66

Nyang, S. A. S., 43

Nyasalanders, 90

Nyerere, J., 38

Obote, M., 97

O'Connell, J., 99

Odinga, O., 85

Olorunsola, V. A., 102

Olson, M., 103

One-party ideology, 55, 72, 74, 110

Opposition, and factionalism, 86-88; in military regime, 126

Optimism, decline of, 10-11; origins of, 2-3

Order, political, 1-13; survival related to, 5, 11

Organizational development, patterns in, 33-39, 44, 51

Pakistan, civil service in, 120, 122-123, 130; military regime in, 96, 110, 115, 118, 120, 128, 129; patrimonialism in, 54

Pakistan Basic Democracies System, 111, 118-119, 122-123, 127, 128

Palace bureaucratic structures, 53, 54, 73

Panter-Brick, S. K., 128

Park Chung-hee, President, 117, 121-122, 126, 128

Parochialism, 21, 58, 66, 110

Parti Démocratique de Côte d'Ivoire (PDCI), 34-35, 36, 54, 55, 62, 63, 101

Parti Démocratique de Guinée, 38

Participation of masses, military view of, 110-111

Particularism, and identity, 13; in middle-class associations, 24, 26; military view of, 110, 111, 127; and modernization, 7; in nationalist movement, 38; persistence of, 21; in rural organizations, 27, 29; and social change, 6; and tradition, 7, 13

Party machines. *See* Machine politics

Patrimonialism, 53-55, 56, 62-63, 67, 71, 79-88, 100; in military regimes, 96, 116, 130

Patronage, 53-54, 55, 57; conflicts over, 67-68; and linkage between center and periphery, 60-64; in military regimes, 118

Patron-client relationships, 6, 32-33, 43-44, 60, 62, 103; changes in, 27; cleavages affecting, 93; communal appeals to, 91-92; and patrimonialism, 54

Pauker, G., 104

PDCI. *See Parti Démocratique de Côte d'Ivoire*

PDG. *See Parti Démocratique de Guinée*

147

Peasant movements, 27-31
Penetration of institutions, 59
People's Action Party, in Singapore, 83, 100
People's National Party, in Sierra Leone, 39, 87, 91
People's Party, in Sierra Leone. *See* Sierra Leone People's Party
Periphery, political, 57-59; bypassing of, 92; lines of authority in, 67-68; in military regimes, 124-128; status hierarchy in, 67; weakening of, 64, 73
Perlmutter, A., 104
Personal relationships, and center-periphery linkages, 68; communal appeals to, 91-92; complex sets of, 70; elites linked by, 53, 55, 60-64; and factionalism, 83-84; in military regimes, 116-117, 120, 124-125, 126; networks of, 94, 103; and patrimonialism, 53
Personalism, effects of, 79
Philippines, 28, 63
Pinkney, R., 127, 130, 131
Pluralism, military view of, 110
PNP. *See* People's National Party
Political development. *See* Development
Political elites, authority extended by, 10; conflicts among, 68-69; relationships to military regimes, 115-116, 117-118, 129; tenuous coalitions of, 52-57
Political machines. *See* Machine politics
Politicians, military view of, 109-112
Powell, G. B., 12, 134, 138
Powell, J. D., 43
Pratt, R. C., 139
Price, R. M., 104
Primordialism, effects of, 58, 72, 79, 91, 92, 101-102
Protest movements, 22, 23-31; linkage to nationalist parties, 37-38; and rural politics, 26-31; tenuous unity of, 41; and urban politics, 23-26
Psychological factors, in nationalism, 15-16, 17, 20, 21
Punjab, 13, 38, 43, 45, 92, 101, 102
Purges, by military regimes, 115, 117
Putnam, R. D., 103
Pye, L., 12, 19, 41, 45, 104, 128, 138

Quandt, W. B., 100

Ranking and authority, conflicts over, 67
Rebellions, by peasants, 28-29
Reciprocity relationships, 60-61, 83; in military regimes, 118, 126
Recruitment of experts, in military regimes, 119-120, 130
Reforms, promoted by middle-class associations, 24, 25
Religion, and peasant movements, 29-30
Religious groups, 25, 38, 43
Resistance movements, primary, 22
Resource allocations, 50, 57; central control over, 60-65; in military regimes, 126; and political conflict, 50, 57
Resources of government, limitations in, 9, 11, 50, 51, 67, 77, 83, 88
Revivalism, 30, 38, 43
Revolutionary Command Council, in Egypt, 112
Richards, A., 72
Rif tribesmen, 88
Riggs, F. W., 12, 100
Rokkan, S., 102
Rose, R., 102
Rosenthal, D. B., 44
Rotberg, R. I., 43
Roth, G., 71
Rothchild, D., 89, 102
Rudebeck, L., 44
Rudolph, L. I., 12, 42, 74, 102
Rudolph, S. H., 12, 42, 74, 102
Rural politics, and protest movements, 26-31
Rustow, D., 113, 128, 129, 138
Rwanda, communal conflicts in, 93
Ryan, S., 74

Sakdalist rebellion, in Philippines, 28
Saya San rebellion, in Burma, 28, 29
Scott, J. C., 42, 74, 92, 101, 103, 136, 138
Seal, A., 42
Segmentation, and conflict, 79, 100; and factionalism, 84; of nationalist movement, 35-36, 50; of political institutions, 8, 13
Senegal, 32, 35-36, 68, 74, 98, 139
Senghor regime, in Senegal, 54, 68, 98

Shepperson, G., 43
Shils, E., 6, 13, 70
Shore, E., 54, 72
Sierra Leone, 71, 100; alliances in,
  52-53; communalism in, 91;
  decentralization in, 80; factional
  conflict in, 83; military regime in,
  112; nationalist movement in, 38-39;
  opposition parties in, 87; party
  machines in, 62
Sierra Leone People's Party (SLPP),
  39, 52-53, 62, 83, 91
Silcock, T. H., 82, 100
Singapore, 83, 100
Sinhala Maha Sabha, 52
Sisson, R., 42, 101
Sklar, R. L., 44, 91, 102
Skurnik, W. A. E., 44, 45, 105
SLPP. See Sierra Leone People's Party
Small, Pa, 31
Smith, M. G., 13
Smock, A. C., 103, 127, 131
Social change, affecting traditional
  groups, 6, 13; differential impact of,
  22; as dysrhythmic process, 5, 13;
  erratic character of, 5-6; holistic view
  of, 5, 21; and instability, 75, 76;
  management of, 3-4, 5; and
  modernization, 3, 22; and
  nationalism, 16-17, 39; and new
  particularisms, 6; and patron-client
  relationships, 32-33; resistance to, 5;
  substructural, 5, 13
Social groups, cleavages in, see
  Cleavages; interactions in, managed
  by institutions, 4; mobilization of, see
  Mobilization; and opposition, 87
Somalia, 53, 97, 105
Southeast Asia, 73, 103, 104;
  cooperatives in, 31; patron-client
  bonds in, 6; religious movements in,
  30
Spoils. See Patronage
Srinivas, M. N., 102
Staniland, M., 86, 101
Status, hierarchy, in periphery, 67
Stepan, A., 104
Strikes, and trade union movement, 26
Stryker, R. E., 73, 74, 139
Subnationalism, 58, 66, 72, 102
Substructural change, effects of, 5, 13
Suharto, 97, 117
Sukarno, 48

Sukuma Union, 25, 31, 37
Suleri, Z. A., 129
Sundhaussen, U., 129
Sundkler, B., 30, 43
Support, for military elites, 108-109; for
  military regimes, 118, 125, 126; new
  sources for, 91; for opposition
  parties, 87, 88
Survival, and political order, 5, 11
Symbols, in religious movements, 30

TAA. See Tanganyikan African
  Association
Tamil parties, in Ceylon, 87
Tanganyikan African Association
  (TAA), 24, 25, 31, 37
Tanganyikan African National Union,
  (TANU), 37-38, 69-70, 81
TANU. See Tanganyikan African
  National Union
Tanzania, 13, 42, 45, 60, 71, 73, 74, 81,
  100, 139
Tax riots, in Sierra Leone, 39
Thailand, 53, 54, 63, 72, 82, 100
Timbuktu, linkage politics in, 38
Togo, military in, 98
Tordoff, W., 74
Touré, S., 38, 44, 45, 54, 110
Trade Union Congress, in Ghana, 82
Trade unions. See Union activity
Traditional groups, 3, 5, 12; and
  center-periphery cohesion, 61, 62;
  conflicts with center, 66; and
  cooperative societies, 31; and
  decentralization, 80-81; and identity,
  93; in military regimes, 127; and
  nationalist movement, 22; and
  particularism, 7, 13; persistence of,
  32-33; resurgence of, 41; social
  change affecting, 6, 13, 76;
  Westernized elites in, 24-25
Trager, F. N., 73
Tribal associations, 25, 38, 39
Tribal identity, 90, 91, 101, 102
Tunisia, 24, 44
Turkey, military regime in, 113

Uganda, 97, 102
Underdevelopment, as chronic
  condition, 11; and political process,
  4-10; time span of, 4; as transitory
  state, 4
Union activities, 26, 42, 74; military

149

view of, 111; and nationalist
movement, 38
Union Progressiste Sénégalaise, 68
United Ghana Farmers' Council, 69, 82
United Gold Coast Convention, 20
United National Party, in Ceylon, 52,
60, 71, 84
United Progressive Party, in Sierra
Leone, 39
Upper Volta, 32, 97, 105
UPS. *See Union Progressiste
Sénégalaise*
Urban politics, and protest
movements, 23-26
Urwin, D., 102
Usury, growth of, 28

Van Doorn, J., 104, 128
Verba, S., 72
Village economy, changes in, 27-28
Violence, urban, 22
Von der Mehden, F. R., 103, 104
Von Vorys, K., 128, 130

Wallerstein, I., 102
Warren, W. M., 42
Waterbury, J., 71, 73
Weber, M., 53, 71
Weiner, M., 65, 73, 74, 101, 130, 136,
138, 139
Welch, C., 12, 105, 107, 108, 128, 129

West Africa, 45, 71, 73; nationalism in,
35, 41; one-party states of, 55
Western ideas, affecting nationalist
elites, 21, 22; affecting patron-client
relationships, 32
Western nations, economic
penetration by, 27, 28; political
development in, 1, 2, 12; view of
nationalism, 16-17
Westernized elites, associations
organized by, 23-26; in traditional
communities, 24-25
Whang, I-J., 130
Whitaker, C. S., 13, 73, 100
Willame, J. C., 71, 128, 130
Willner, A. R., 108, 128
Wolf, E., 27, 28, 42, 43
Wolpe, H., 99, 102, 103
Woodward, C. A., 45, 71, 73, 101
Wriggins, W. H., 45, 133, 138

Yalman, N., 129
Young, C., 23, 42, 43, 102, 103
Young Tunisians, 24
Youth groups, aspirations of, 76-77

Zaire, role of experts in, 120
Ziring, L., 129
Zolberg, A., 34, 36, 44, 45, 70, 71, 72,
73, 98, 99, 100, 128, 136, 139

3 4 5 6 7 8 9 10 11 12 13 14 15   88 87 86 85 84 83 82